THE NEW

BRAINBOOSTER

THE NEW

BRAINBOOSTER

Six Hours to
Rapid Learning
and Remembering

ROBERT W. FINKEL

Chaion, NY

Copyright © 1983, 1991, 2011 by Robert W. Finkel

This edition published in 2011
by Chaion Analytics

Library of Congress Cataloging-in-Publication Data
Finkel, Robert W.
The new brainbooster: six hours to rapid learning and remembering
/ Robert W. Finkel.
p. cm.
Rev. ed. of: Brain booster. c1983.
Includes bibliographical references and index.
ISBN-13: 978-0615448237
1. Mnemonics.   2. Learning, Psychology of.   I. Finkel, Robert W.
Brain booster.   II. Title.   III. Title: New brainbooster.
BF385.F54   1991
153.1—dc20   91-13281
CIP

Printed in the United States of America

2   4   6   8   10   9   7   5   3   1

We are pleased to credit the following sources of reprinted material:
Excerpts from A. R. Luria, *The Mind of a Mnemonist*. Translated from the Russian
by Lynn Solotaroff. © 1968 by Basic Books, Inc. By permission of Basic Books, Inc.,
and by Jonathon Cape Ltd.
Article by Mitchel L. Zoler, "Touch, Taste, and the Desire to Eat." This material
originally appeared in *Science Digest*, April, 1981. Reprinted by permission of the
author.
Excerpt on the development of language and speech from Gloria J. Borden and
Katherine S. Harris, *Speech Science Primer*. © 1980 by the Williams and Wilkins
Co., Baltimore. Reprinted by permission.
The article on "The Black Death" is extracted from *The Man-Made World* published by McGraw-Hill, © 1971 by Polytechnic Institute of Brooklyn. Reprint
publication of this article is not an endorsement by the original copyright owner.
Excerpts from an article by W. Langer, "The Black Death." This originally
appeared in *Scientific American*, February, 1964. By permission of W. H. Freeman
and Company.
We are thankful to the International Paper Company for permission to reprint an
article from the "Power of the Printed Word" program, "How to Write With Style"
by Kurt Vonnegut.

**Lovingly Dedicated
to Carla**

■

CONTENTS

■

ABOUT THIS
UNIQUE BOOK

■

This is a book of practical techniques for learning and remembering. It shows you how to learn more, faster—with clear, lasting recall. You can acquire the techniques easily, quickly, and use them immediately.

Studies in brain physiology, memory, educational psychology, and a host of other cognitive sciences reveal that we have awesome mental potential—and that at best we use very little of it. Fortunately, the cognitive sciences indicate ways to reach your untapped powers to help you understand and assimilate information and ideas. This book shows you how.

The New Brainbooster is your instruction manual. It will teach you to deepen your comprehension, to absorb information rapidly, to remember much more, much longer, and to penetrate problems.

The techniques are useful because they are simple and easy to learn. They work by changing your view of information to forms your mind can easily digest. Some techniques are ancient theatrical devices with a new respectability bestowed by the cognitive sciences. Others are related to the practices of various expert thinkers such as mnemonists, problem solvers, scientists, and other intellectual athletes.

This book explains how the diverse techniques arise from their common roots—a few basic elements such as the telescopic approach and the method of substitute images. Moreover, these elements are derived from basic scientific findings or well-tested practice and experience.

Many of the techniques presented here—the telescopic approach to organization, the S.O.S. technique for problem solving, the method for mental recording of lectures and films, and the technique of animated digits for remembering numbers—reflect common practices used by experts.

A special feature of these techniques is that they can be used immediately, usually after one reading. The original versions of many powerful techniques required much practice to master, which no doubt limited the use of learning techniques in education. The new techniques make it easier to learn how to learn.

The New Brainbooster guides you step by step. It shows you the memory systems of great mnemonists: how to remember words, terms, and foreign vocabularies; recall a dozen people after a single introduction; retain telephone numbers, dates, prices, and numbers of any length. And these techniques are joined with principles of mental organization to create rapid learning techniques: how to learn diagrams, processes, and facts; read deeply and remember readings in graphic detail; improve writing, teaching, and public speaking; solve problems; absorb lectures, presentations, and films, even without notes—and more. Best of all, this book shows you can enjoy learning quickly and easily.

PART

I

■

THE

FUNDAMENTALS

■

The first three chapters provide
a quick introduction to the
fundamental techniques for
rapid learning and
remembering.

■

1

■

ABOUT
TECHNIQUES

■

Simple, easily learned
techniques use organization,
visualization, and
association

■

Joan Conte is the most successful premedical student in her college. During her class in organic chemistry, the other students take notes feverishly. The whir of tape recorders blends with the professor's monotone, and chemical hieroglyphics cover the blackboard. After the lecture Jan holds court in the student lounge where, without a textbook or notes, she recreates and interprets the lecture, even drawing complex chemical structures from memory. The other students usually take hours of additional study to approach Joan's mastery of the material.

A young executive, Bart Welkson, wanted an important position in a New York concern. His chances seemed poor because he was competing with more experienced people.

After a long wait, Bart received a ninety-page company report and an invitation to be interviewed by the firm's executive board on the following day. The company vice-president apologized at the interview for not sending the report early enough for a close examination. Bart replied that he knew the report well—just mention any page number at random, and, without looking, he would describe the contents and offer his thoughts about them. The interviewers took the bait, and Bart verified his claim, page after page. The wide-eyed board members offered him the position before he left the room.

Such feats of learning and remembering appear virtually superhuman, but Joan and Bart are very much like you and me. They were not born with this exceptional ability—they developed it. And you can, too.

THE CHARACTERISTICS OF LEARNING TECHNIQUES

Your learning abilities can soar with simple techniques that use organization, visualization, and association. These are not traditional study methods or exercises in willpower and determination, but far more effective measures that are easily learned and that can be applied immediately to your studies or work.

This seems incredible to people who believe that the ability to learn is a fixed inherited trait and that only hard work, attention, and discipline can make a difference in how quickly or thoroughly we learn. That attitude is widespread, although it is discredited by research in psychology and education and by everyday experience. Factors such as cultural background, format of presentation, interest in the subject matter, personality, and even humor have significant impacts on learning. Perhaps it is not surprising, then, that techniques that orga-

4

nize and improve your perception of information can and do increase comprehension and memory.

A learning technique is a procedure for organizing or interpreting information to improve understanding or recall. For example, a map may be learned by mentally shifting its elements into an easily recognized pattern. The actual map is then remembered as a perturbation of the simplified map. A more familiar technique is to form acronyms—the word HOMES reminds us of the great lakes (Huron, Ontario, Michigan, Erie, and Superior). Still another technique is identifying topic sentences to improve reading comprehension. All these are useful aids to learning and are restricted forms of the more fundamental techniques presented in this book.

WHY TECHNIQUES WORK

We are told that we use only a minuscule fraction of our mental capabilities. How can we have such enormous potential and realize so little of it? Why are we unable to learn much more, much faster, despite our best efforts?

These questions invite speculation. I suspect that the information in "book learning" is not in a form most easily grasped and retained by our brains—brains that are best designed for more fundamental or primitive functions. For example, our verbal memory is less powerful than our primordial visual memory. I suspect that the spectacular success of learning techniques is partly due to their encoding of information into forms found most "digestible" by the brain.

As you use these techniques, you will find yourself learning through vivid visualization, association, and organization. Visualization is employed to tap the powerful visual memory mechanism. Association links old and new information in a manner we seem neurologically well suited to absorb. And, perhaps most important, well-organized material is easily understood and easily recalled.

Another reason for the effectiveness of learning techniques is that they create a state of attentiveness. When you use techniques, you interact with the material. This is a creative, interesting process that fosters high levels of concentration.

SOURCES OF LEARNING TECHNIQUES

Television reaches around the earth, robots run our factories, we probe outer space, conquer myriad diseases, and increase life expectancy. Advances in sports physiology enable a new generation of champions to topple record after record. How incongruous it is that the usual advice we receive for learning in the space age amounts to "pay attention, rehearse often, and try hard."

We *do* know how to improve learning ability. Recent findings in brain physiology, nutrition, educational psychology, and memory research all suggest applications that can improve your ability to learn. Moreover, we have a great legacy of learning techniques; they are practiced regularly by various professionals. People with trained memories, mnemonists, easily recall hundreds of items in minutes. Engineers and physical scientists "read" equations and crack problems with a barrage of techniques. Many artists paint complex and detailed scenes without having the subject in view. Some public speakers lecture at length without notes. Seasoned specialists of all kinds devour dense reports in their fields quickly and easily.

These impressive skills are "tricks of the trade" that are usually not taught formally, but are learned by experience and observation. Although they are very diverse, they are all products of mental organization, visualization, and association—the common denominators of learning techniques.

I have unabashedly borrowed, altered, and developed learning techniques from all these sources. Some techniques, then, are based on scientific findings, and others are rooted in experience and practice. I have distilled the techniques to a few that are most effective and most easily mastered.

ON READING THIS BOOK

The chapters of this book fit into one of three categories: (1) central techniques that have the widest utility; (2) special applications of these central techniques (sometimes including peripheral techniques); and (3) general information.

With *The New Brainbooster* you begin your rapid learning immediately. You can master the basics and put them to work in a few hours.

Most of the chapters include examples and exercises. I urge you to work through these. It requires some effort, but the reward is an ability to learn more, faster, and thoroughly.

2

■

THE

FUNDAMENTALS

■

The secrets of rapid learning and remembering in a nutshell

■

This chapter reveals the secrets of rapid learning and remembering in a nutshell. Most of the following is a brief exercise that I will guide you through step by step. Here you learn the basics of the major techniques that are used throughout.

A reading passage outlining our techniques is given in the next section. You can easily remember the important points and terms with some study. However, to get the feeling of using these techniques, simply read the following section casually and comfortably. Following that, I will walk you through techniques for learning and remembering the reading passage.

THE FUNDAMENTALS

A READING PASSAGE

Basics of Rapid Learning

Imagination is the key to rapid learning and remembering. You can easily digest a story that is simply organized, vividly illustrated, and that relates to familiar facts and details. The idea is to use your imagination to impose these characteristics on any article. This can be done with a few techniques for mentally organizing, visualizing, and associating the information.

The cognitive sciences show that organization, visualization, and association are important—even essential—to learning. These features are incorporated in the three most fundamental techniques: telescopic thinking, substitute imagery, and memory chains. Most other techniques are variations and combinations of these.

Organization is often the most important step in learning difficult or complex material. We use a "telescopic" approach to organization where we first see information in a very simple outline form and then focus on successive layers of increasing detail. For example, when learning the basics of the circulatory system, we first focus on the system as consisting of only three units: body, heart, and lungs. That basic outline then is elaborated by a first level of detail—perhaps the major connections between the units. Successive layers of detail then might include the chambers of the heart, major arteries and veins, and so on until the desired level of accuracy is reached. Notice that we begin with the *least* detailed and most general items first.

This layered approach is a hallmark of expert thinking. It seems so simple and ordinary that we are likely to underestimate its power. Applying it purposefully to new material leads to dramatic learning. Telescoping can be applied di-

9

rectly to reading, learning maps and processes, writing, and much more. It is also the backbone of a structured approach to mathematical problem solving.

Visualization and association are usually used together to relieve the time and tedium of rote memorization. It is no accident that visualization and association are standard tools for professional memory experts; humans are supremely well equipped for visual thinking. According to one estimate, about 60 percent of the brain contributes to the visual system. Contrast that with the reality that most schooling supplies information in verbal forms. The brain also has an enormous capability for association, and it is commonplace for people to remember dozens of connected items and events without difficulty.

Substitute imagery and *memory chains* together are the basic techniques using visualization and association. Substitute imagery works by imagining simple pictures to stand for significant words or ideas. For example, an image of Uncle Sam can represent the United States. The term substitute imagery might be symbolized by a submarine, which has nothing to do with the term other than share a syllable, *sub*. However, *sub* is enough of a cue to remind us of substitute imagery. Some useful applications include remembering people, learning English and foreign vocabulary, and learning technical and medical terminology.

Memory chains help us to remember a sequence by converting it into a meaningful, connected series of events or images. As a simple example, you might memorize a shopping list by imagining your friends arriving one at a time each with a listed item. Of course, your friends have no actual relation to the items, but the "story" makes the list memorable. Chaining is usually used with substitute imagery to relieve the drudgery of rote memorization.

TRY IT

Now you can glimpse the power of brainbooster techniques by using them on the reading passage. Simply follow my instructions step by step.

Some of these instructions seem silly or superfluous for this simple assignment. Bear with me because a similar approach will be invaluable for much longer, more complex material.

1. The passage can be separated into parts labeled *organization, visualization,* and *association*. Use the acronym OVA to remind you of these elements. The first paragraph indicates that we use imagination to impose organization, visualization, and association, so a visual map of the basic organization is as follows:

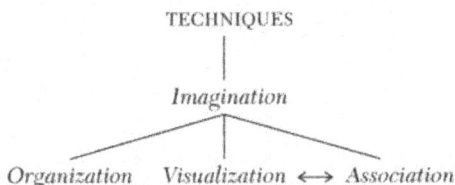

TECHNIQUES
|
Imagination

Organization   Visualization ⟷ Association

Notice that *visualization* and *association* are linked to indicate that these usually are used together. Commit the diagram to memory so that you can look away and mentally sketch it.

2. Now note that we use the telescopic approach for organization, substitute imagery for visualization, and memory chains for association. Use objects to remind you of these basic techniques: a telescope, a submarine, and a chain. Include these on the diagram:

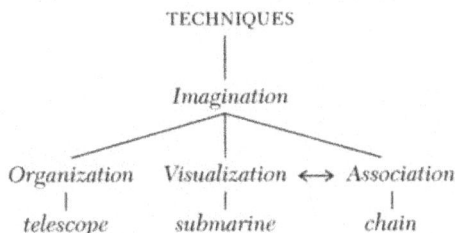

TECHNIQUES
|
Imagination

Organization   Visualization ⟷ Association
| | |
telescope   submarine   chain

Visualize the objects vividly and be sure you can mentally reproduce the original diagram and the new additions.

3. Telescoping is the technique of seeing information in layers from the *least* to the *most* detail. Your mind's eye can remind you of this definition by seeing a layer cake where you must remember that each layer represents more detail. I attached *layer cake* to *telescope* on the diagram.

Substitute imagery is the technique of replacing words or ideas with simple pictures. The term substitute image is almost self-explanatory, so we can leave the definition off our diagram. An example of a substitute image is Uncle Sam representing the United States, so I attached *Uncle Sam* to the diagram under *submarine*.

Memory chains are artificial stories that connect information so that one item reminds you of the next. The word *story* will remind you of this; use your imagination to have a storybook stand for the word *story* and include it on the diagram.

Look at the current diagram. Associate the new details by seeing (a) the telescope sticking into the cake, (b) Uncle Sam climbing out of the submarine, and (c) a storybook hanging from the chain. See these clearly and then recall the diagram in stages 1, 2, and 3.

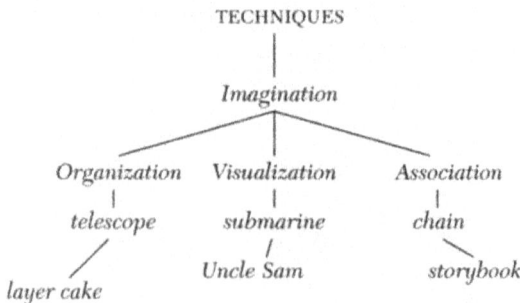

TECHNIQUES
|
Imagination

Organization   *Visualization*   *Association*
| | |
telescope   *submarine*   *chain*
/ | \
layer cake   *Uncle Sam*   *storybook*

4. Finally, attach some of the applications of telescoping and substitute imagery to the diagram. Maps, reading, and writing are applications of telescoping, and they can be represented by a map, eyeglasses, and a pen. Clearly imagine eyeglasses and a pen on a map and remember that the glasses stand for reading and the pen for writing. Connect this scene to the telescope by seeing it through the telescope.

Some of the applications of substitute imagery are learning names, vocabulary, and medical terminology. Resolve to let *names* be represented by a name tag, *vocabulary* by a dictionary, and *medical terminology* by a skeleton. Picture vividly a skeleton wearing a name tag and reading a dictionary—it doesn't need to make good sense to work. Be sure you can recall what each item represents. The scene can be related to the *submarine* portion of the diagram by thinking that Uncle Sam gave the dictionary to the skeleton.

Look at the final diagram. Locate the new details on the diagram by seeing (a) the map with glasses and pen through the telescope, and (b) Uncle Sam giving a dictionary to a skeleton sporting a name tag. See these clearly and then recall the diagram in stages 1, 2, 3, and 4.

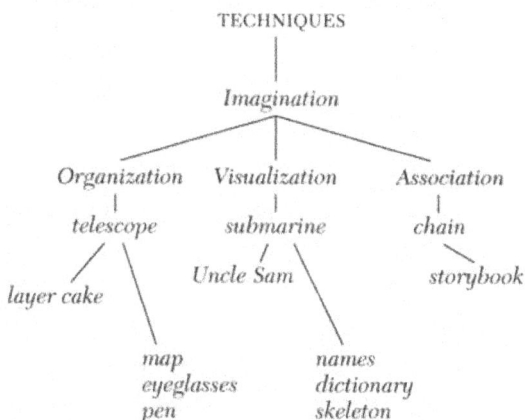

TECHNIQUES

Imagination

Organization   *Visualization*   *Association*

telescope   submarine   chain

layer cake   *Uncle Sam*   storybook

map   names
eyeglasses   dictionary
pen   skeleton

REVIEW QUESTIONS

Answer the following review questions without looking at the passage or diagram.

1. Our techniques use imagination to impose what three features on information?
2. Name the primary technique associated with each of the three features above.
3. Telescoping is ordering information from the (a) more to less important, (b) less to more important, (c) most to least detail, (d) least to most detail, (e) top to bottom
4. Name three important applications of telescoping.
5. Which are most often used together? (a) telescoping and substitute imagery, (b) telescoping and memory chaining, (c) substitute imagery and memory chaining, (d) mapping and substitute imagery, (e) mapping and memory chaining
6. Uncle Sam is used as an example of (a) telescoping, (b) mapping, (c) substitute imagery, (d) memory chaining
7. List three applications of substitute imagery.
8. Using a story to recall a sequence is called (a) telescoping, (b) mapping, (c) substitute imagery, (d) memory chaining

The answers are given at the end of this chapter. You may be confident enough to *know* you answered everything correctly. Very likely you can talk or write about the subject in detail without further rehearsal. That is the experience of using brainbooster techniques.

WHAT YOU ACCOMPLISHED

You used each of the major techniques in the exercise. A map of the passage began with the most general basic organization and progressed to levels of more detail. Clearly, this is telescoping.

Substitute imagery was applied to terms and ideas on the map when you replaced them with concrete images; a pen stood for writing and a layer cake represented the idea of layering material in increasing detail.

Memory chains linked otherwise unrelated items together so that the list *names, vocabulary, medical terminology* was converted to a bizarre scene with a skeleton wearing a name tag and reading a dictionary.

Of course, I fed you my own telescopic organization and substitute imagery. You will soon do the telescoping and imagery for yourself and your learning and remembering will be even more effective.

ANSWERS TO REVIEW QUESTIONS

1. organization, visualization, association
2. telescoping, substitute imagery, memory chains
3. d
4. learning maps, reading, writing
5. c
6. c
7. names, vocabulary, medical terminology
8. d

3

∎

QUESTIONS
AND ANSWERS

∎

Most frequently asked
questions about the
techniques

∎

▌demonstrate techniques to audiences by helping them learn a map of an industrial park. Minutes after seeing how to expand their thinking, the participants give directions from any particular building to any other—without looking at the map. They are amused and rightfully impressed by their own powers.

As a climax to the demonstration, I distribute copies of a current news magazine such as *Time* or *Newsweek* (or an annual report, for a business audience). People then call out random page numbers, and I summarize the articles on these pages from memory, describing even the photographs and layouts.

The demonstration is followed by a question period, and the following questions are based on these sessions. Many of the points raised here are discussed throughout the book, but it is useful to anticipate these questions now.

Q: Do you have a "trick" memory?

A: I have a normal memory, probably much like yours. I often cannot remember where I parked my car, and I forget my own telephone number—maybe this qualifies as a trick memory!

Q: Is this primarily a memory improvement course?

A: Memory techniques are an important part of this subject, but we are most concerned with learning in general. This includes cognitive and conceptual skills as well as memory: how to extract ideas from reading and listening, how to solve problems, how to take notes, and how to organize thoughts are all addressed.

The memory aspects are certainly the most showy and impressive. After all, you cannot demonstrate learning without also demonstrating memory. Techniques that specifically assist memory are called *mnemonics* or *mnemonic devices*. I used several of these to remember the demonstration magazine.

Incidentally, I did not memorize the demonstration magazine word for word as you might memorize a poem or a script. I prefer to say that I *learned* it, insofar as I know the central points and recall the most important details. Nevertheless, the demonstration is always seen as a memory feat.

Q: Will I be able to learn an entire magazine by page number?

A: Yes. It involves nothing more than an application of several techniques. Professional mnemonists do similar things for theatrical impact onstage.

Q: What is the quality of this kind of learning? How long will it be remembered?

A: No doubt you fear that learning with techniques is too easy and somehow the quality of learning must be inferior. Perhaps it is rapidly forgotten or easily confused.

The opposite is true. You will probably remember the demonstration map for weeks, although I can hardly imagine a more useless bit of information. The bold impressions made with techniques persist longer and more clearly than memories achieved though rote.

Q: Are the techniques based on willpower or positive thinking?

A: No. The techniques are based on principles of organization, visualization, and association. When you use techniques, you are improving your view of information so that it is easier to understand and easier to remember.

Q: How long will it take before I can use the techniques?

A: These techniques can be used immediately. The time you invest is the time you spend reading the book or participating in the seminar.

It takes most people about six hours to become rapid learners in all but a few specialized areas. My seminars usually run for six hourly sessions and participants report big gains after two or three sessions.

Of course, you improve your learning skills as you use them. You can practice on material you would otherwise learn by standard means. Usually, learning with a new technique will be as fast or faster than the conventional approach, even in the first application.

Q: What subjects are suitable for rapid learning techniques?

A: Learning can be accelerated in most subjects. Techniques are effective for reading, listening, taking notes, solving problems, and the recall of facts, terms, and numbers. These are certainly important skills for a majority of subject areas.

Naturally, the usefulness of the techniques varies with the subjects or topics. There are some topics that elude the application of techniques. For instance, I don't yet have good suggestions for treating foreign grammars, although techniques work nicely for foreign vocabulary.

Q: I am a teacher. Can learning techniques be used to improve instruction?

A: Yes. A number of rapid learners use techniques in the classroom with exceptional success. A chapter on teaching with techniques is included in the book.

Q: Will this course make me more intelligent?

A: I think so, although many people disagree. They regard intelligence as inflexibly fixed by genetics, and they describe it with a single number, the I.Q. If this view is realistic, no amount of learning and no mental skill you develop—however extraordinary—have the smallest effect on your intelligence.

You and I recognize intelligence when we see it: the abilities to learn, to create, to think through problems, to understand concepts, to remember, and so on. And most of these attributes can be improved with techniques.

Q: What is the level of instruction?

A: Most of the information is aimed at the level of the reading public, which I assume to be bright, but unfamiliar with any learning techniques.

Q: Do the techniques become habitual? Do you use them all the time?

A: No. You need to make a conscious effort to apply most of the techniques. Everyday reading and listening usually don't warrant this effort. You can "switch on" techniques whenever the demands to learn and remember become pressing.

Many former students and clients report that they went through a long period during which they mixed the techniques with their old study methods. This is a very good procedure, because a lot of mental energy is spent in applying new techniques. Mixing new and old methods gives you time to become comfortable and confident with the new techniques. You don't give up common sense just because you learn some powerful techniques.

Q: Is any special ability required?

A: No. Normal individuals learn the techniques without difficulty. Only rarely does someone claim to be unable to visualize events or to organize certain material. Some very bright people with learning disabilities also have trouble using several of the techniques. But these are exceptions.

Most people are quite unaware that they have immense intellectual potential. Techniques enable you to realize some of your latent powers.

PART

II

RAPID
LEARNING

Part II looks more deeply into
the three fundamental
techniques: substitute imagery,
memory chaining, and
telescopic thinking.

4

■

YOUR

MIND'S EYE

■

Two central memory
techniques: the memory
chain and substitute images

■

In the next few minutes you will learn how to memorize long lists after reading them just once! You will use a *memory chain* method based upon principles of visualization and association. This technique and the related *substitute images* technique are the foundation for most memory courses and exhibitions.

THE MEMORY CHAIN

A memory chain is a device for memorizing a sequence of items. The idea is to have the first item remind you of the second, the second remind you of the third, and so on through the list. You can do this easily by creating striking mental images that link each new item to the last item.

The technique is demonstrated on the following list. Please resist the temptation to memorize the list without reading the instructions. This would just waste your energy and prove nothing. Instead, follow the instructions next to each item and work your way down the list. Don't hurry, but don't stop to rehearse either.

Item	Instructions
egg	Imagine a huge egg.
shoe	To associate *shoe* with *egg*, imagine an animated shoe kicking a hole in the egg. Visualize this clearly for a moment or two.
car	Link *car* with *shoe* by imagining that the shoe grows into a car and develops headlights and wheels. Don't be deterred by the absurdity of the image: see it clearly and move to the next item.
tree	Associate *tree* by visualizing a tree sprouting from the hood of a car.
hot dog	Continue on your own by making any fantastic association to connect *hot dog* with *tree*. Visualize this clearly.
apple	Continue on your own. Make the association unusual. Visualize it clearly and go on.
cigar	Continue on your own. Trust yourself—do not rehearse earlier associations.
flower	Continue on your own. It is most important to visualize your association for a moment.
chair	Continue on your own. Almost any bizarre association will do, if you can visualize it.
desk	"Ah," you say, *desk* and *chair* are naturally associated, so this will be easy to remember. Not so. It is easier to remember items that have unusual associations (like *tree* and *hot dog*). Use your imagination to distort the relation between desk and chair (for example, by exaggerating the size of one).
chalk	Continue on your own.
watch	Continue on your own.

Now repeat the entire list from memory—then repeat it backward!

SOME FEATURES OF THE TECHNIQUE

Very likely you are impressed by your ability to remember the list so easily and accurately. Your associations gave meaning to the list, and your visualizations made the associations memorable and vivid. The memory chain technique uses your natural abilities to learn by association and visualization rather than by plodding repetition. Your creativity and imagination replace deadening drill.

Despite these facts, people usually ask me how long they will remember a list that was learned in such an "artificial" manner (implying that learning by rote is "natural"). You may expect to remember the list for days or even weeks without conscious rehearsal. In any event, you will remember it much longer than if you had learned it by rote.

Associations are most effective when they are imaginative and unusual. A tree bearing hot dog "fruit" and a shoe sporting headlights are easily remembered. Many people are uncomfortable using these silly associations. They feel that frivolous thoughts are undignified, even though they are completely private. If you are one of the few people who cannot overcome this attitude, you can still imagine less dramatic or silly associations, but they will require somewhat more attention and rehearsal.

You can form strong associations by imposing one or more of the following features:

1. Unusual sizes or numbers (for example, a huge egg or hundreds of tiny apples).
2. Unusual materials (for example, a bird made of bricks or wheels made of watches).

3. Dynamic motion, including growth, sex, or violence (for example, a shoe kicking an egg).

The first item in a list should be particularly outstanding because it has no prior association.

The memory chain technique requires that you visualize an association clearly before you continue to the next item. This is the most important step in forming a memory chain—you must picture the association.

Now you can form a memory chain for another list. You'll see that your own associations are the most effective. Once you have pictured an association vividly, trust your memory and continue to the next association. Even when you form a memory chain slowly, you are memorizing many times faster than you possibly can without a technique.

EXERCISE

Memorize the following list using the memory chain technique.

foot	key	tire	frying pan
wall	book	carrot	candle
dog	matches	eyeglasses	nose

A MAN WITH A BOUNDLESS MEMORY

One of the greatest memories ever documented belonged to a Russian newspaper reporter, Solomon Veniaminovich Shceresheveskii. Experiments showed that he had no difficulty reproducing word series and number sequences of any length. Although he memorized thousands of series, Sheresheveskii could recall any one upon request fifteen or sixteen years later. His memory had no apparent limits, either in its capacity or in its permanence.

In the mid 1920s Shereshevskii was nearly thirty, but still unaware that he was in any way unusual—doesn't everyone remember everything they are told? The puzzled reporter was sent by his editor to a psychology laboratory for testing. There he stunned the renowned psychologist A. R. Luria, who began a study of Shereshevskii that lasted nearly thirty years.

Professor Luria's report shows that Shereshevskii's titanic memory was due primarily to his *vivid visual imagery* and *graphic associations*, the very same mechanisms you use in this chapter.

Shereshevskii did not set out to master concrete visualization and association—mastery was forced upon him by a mental quirk. He *had* to visualize every thought in concrete and specific images. His inner world was one of myriad particulars, each with an isolated existence, without patterns, relationships, or generalizations. He said he could only understand what he could visualize.

This strange quirk, which was responsible for his great gift, also placed great limitations on him. Shereshevskii was unable to understand abstractions like "nothing" and "infinity." He had to memorize a predictable sequence of digits with the same concentration he needed for a random number list. He even had great difficulty recognizing people's faces because, as he described:

> They're so changeable. A person's expression depends on his mood and on the circumstances under which you happen to meet him. People's faces are constantly changing; it's the different shades of expression that confuse me and make it so hard to remember faces. (A. R. Luria, *The Mind of a Mnemonist*)

Sometime after Shereshevskii became aware of his powers he brought them to the stage and became a professional mnemonist. He deliberately refined and developed his techniques to make them error-free and to enable him to handle any type of nonsense sequences or passages in unfamiliar foreign languages. He was successful and became quite well known.

A major difference between you and Sheresheveskii is that you have the option to use memory devices, whereas he simply had no choice. There are professional mnemonists today who are free of mental aberrations but who can rival his performances. However, unlike Sheresheveskii, these talented individuals are unlikely to remember trivia forever. Their healthy minds organize information, retaining what seems important and eliminating the mental junk.

This is not the full story of the man-who-remembered-everything. You will have several occasions to learn more about the art of remembering from his case history.

SUBSTITUTE IMAGES

By now you recognize that your ability to remember long lists of objects is impressive but not very useful. Most of the words, terms, or ideas you want to remember are not visual descriptions. Nevertheless, your technique for remembering objects can be upgraded to help you remember verbal information: simply create mental images that remind you of the original wording.

This technique of substituting graphic images to represent abstract words was essential to mnemonist Sheresheveskii's thinking. When he heard the word *green*, he imagined a green flowerpot; *America* was represented by an image of Uncle Sam; and the word *transcendent* evoked a picture of his teacher looking at a monument. These concrete images served as cues to recall the original words.

You can easily develop this substitute image technique.

Suppose, for example, that a student of political science is to be tested on the basic statistics of several countries. In order to structure the essay answers, the student wants to remember the list of key words given below. Put yourself in the student's situation and follow the instructions next to each word—you will have ample opportunity to create your own imagery later. Use bold, clear, exaggerated images and spend about thirty or forty seconds on each word.

Words	Instructions
location	Imagine an arrow embedded in some *location* on a map. Pay special attention to this image because it begins the sequence.
area (square kilometers)	A square was the first area you studied in school. Visualize a paper square attached like a flag to the arrow. The square represents *area*.
population	Picture hundreds of tiny people emerging from the square. The people represent *population*.
chief cities	The people pour into a city building (representing *cities*) until the building walls bulge. If you think you may need a reminder for *chief*, put a huge fire chief hat on top of the building.
government	Use a crown as a symbol for government, and continue on your own by making a very graphic association with the city building.
manufacturing	Continue on your own by imagining any particular manufactured item: if you decide that it will represent *manufacturing*, it will work. Make a strong link into the crown and proceed.
agriculture	Continue on your own. Use specific items, not a vague scene.
raw materials	Continue on your own.
monetary unit	Continue on your own.

Finally, repeat the list from memory.

SENSE IMPRESSIONS

Educators tell us to involve as many senses as possible when we are studying. When learning new terms, for instance, it helps to hear the term, to speak it, and to write it. It is good advice. This chapter is concerned with visual impressions, and we want to embellish these with other sensory information to make them even stronger memory aids.

Some people taste names, hear pictures, feel smells, and see dancing colors in the sound of a voice. A rare disorder called *synesthesia* includes these and other blurrings between the borders of the senses. Sheresheveskii had such marked synesthesia that he "saw" words and sounds as puffs of steam, animated colored strips, and the like. Professor Luria was not thinking of the most powerful memory in the world when he asked whether Sheresheveskii could find his way home from a testing center. The reply shows the blitz of sensations the mnemonist lived with:

> Come now, how could I possibly forget. After all here is this fence, it has such a salty taste and feels so rough; furthermore it has such a sharp piercing sound. (Ibid.)

Sheresheveskii's synesthesia and his bottomless memory were related. The Russian's visualizations were so bold, so saturated with impressions from every sense, that they were etched deeply in his mind.

This is a way to amplify your own impressions. Dress your mental images with imagined tastes, colors, textures, and sounds. The bolder, the better. After all, the most important step in memory systems is to form vivid images—and various sensory cues intensify them. No one can forget a salty-tasting, rough, shrill fence.

SUMMARY

Memory chain: To remember a list, associate the first item with the second, the second with the third, and so on. Associations are most effective when they are imaginative and unusual. Items of unusual size, unusual material, or having dynamic motion are best remembered. Visualization is the most important step in forming a memory chain; picture each association clearly before continuing to the next item.

Substitute images: To remember words, create concrete images to serve as cues. Your "natural" memory cements the word to the image, however abstract the word may be.

Sense impressions: Embellish visual images with tastes, colors, textures, and sounds. These make images more vivid and memorable.

EXERCISES

1. Memorize the following list using the memory chain and substitute image techniques.

tea	candle	horn	flavor
arm	noise	wonderful	planet
friendship	fish	baseball	cash register

2. As you will see in later chapters, one of the most useful applications of memory chain and substitute image techniques is to memorize *key words*. The key words are reminders of facts and ideas. The list of key words in this exercise should remind you of the central points narrated about Sheresheveskii in this chapter. Memorize the list and see if you remember the associated ideas. (Don't bother to remember the ideas word by word.)

Key Words	Fact or Idea
reporter	Sheresheveskii was a newspaper reporter when his powers were discovered.
no limits	His memory was limitless in capacity and duration.

31

experiments	He was the subject of psychological experiments for nearly thirty years.
techniques	Sharesheveskii used visualization and association.
disorder	He had a disorder that forced him to use imagery.
professional	He became a professional performer of memory feats.
substitute images	Sheresheveskii used concrete images as cues for words.

5

■

TELESCOPIC
THINKING

■

Telescoping: a central
technique for organizing and
learning

■

Years ago I watched an artist paint a portrait of an ordinary woman. I remember that portrait vividly because I saw it evolve in stages from an outline to a detailed picture.

The artist began by sketching an outline of the woman's head. He then marked the placement of her eyes, nose, and mouth. Only after the outline and basic features were formed did he begin to add details, shading, and color. As each detail came into focus, I saw how it related to the whole face. It was easy to remember new features because they were mentally associated with earlier structures.

The evolution of a portrait illustrates the *telescopic technique*—perhaps the best single method for organizing and learning difficult material. Specifically, telescoping is the

33

technique of first treating broad outlines, followed by successive refinement of details. The approach is particularly useful for learning complex processes and lengthy or difficult texts. A number of applications are given in subsequent chapters; here I concentrate on introducing the technique and applying it to diagrams and processes.

THE BASICS OF THE TECHNIQUE

In the telescopic approach to learning, you first view gross features under low magnification. Then you increase the magnification in stages to reveal finer and finer details. The technique may also be seen as a pyramidal approach in which the most fundamental layer—the outline, or the "core"—is a base for successive layers of details. Each stage or layer is clearly associated with the previous stage. When you reconstruct the outline, the details cascade forth with each layer reminding you of the next.

As an example, you can learn the blood flow relationships between the lungs, heart, and body by applying the telescopic technique. The ultimate diagram you need to understand and reproduce is shown in Figure 5.1. As usual, don't bother to see whether you can learn the diagram without

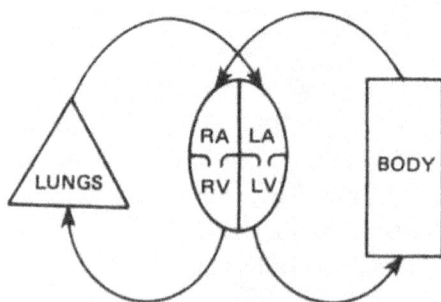

FIGURE 5.1. Circulatory System

techniques—you can do so easily, but your purpose is to follow the instructions closely in order to acquire the technique.

Proceed by drawing some of the most important units in the diagram—in this case the lungs, heart, and body (Figure 5.2). This is the outline stage. Now embellish the drawing by connecting some blood vessels, say those that flow through the left side of the heart (Figure 5.3). Next, add further detail by connecting blood vessels that flow through the right side of the heart (Figure 5.4). Finally, add valves to the heart and identify Right Atrium and Right Ventricle (RA and RV) and Left Atrium and Left Ventricle (LA and LV) as in Figure 5.5.

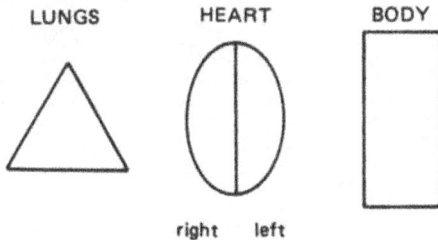

FIGURE 5.2. Three basic elements of the circulatory system: lungs, heart, and body. Notice that right and left correspond to a person facing out of the page. (We begin with the heart split vertically.)

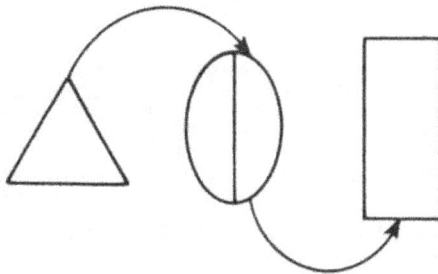

FIGURE 5.3. Fully oxygenated blood flows from the lungs to the heart. The heart pumps this blood to the body.

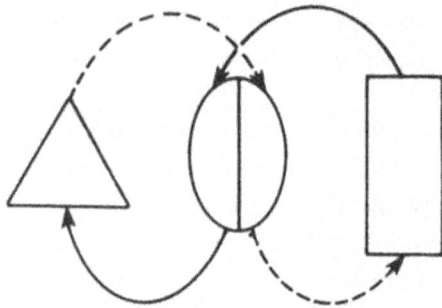

FIGURE 5.4. Blood flowing through the body surrenders its oxygen. This blood returns to the heart and is pumped to the lungs to pick up more oxygen.

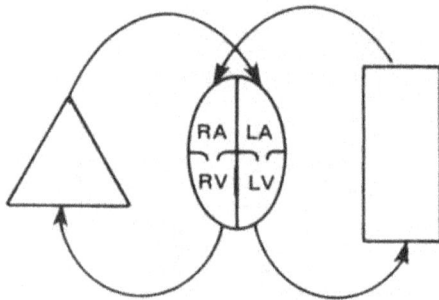

FIGURE 5.5. The heart has four chambers: left atrium (LA), right atrium (RA), left ventricle (LV), and right ventricle (RV).

Rehearse each stage briefly, and be sure to associate each step with the preceding stage. Then draw the complete diagram from memory.

THE REDUCTION PROCESS

In telescoping, information is packaged in layers of increasing detail. Very often, however, the original material does not seem to have layers that are simple enough to grasp quickly.

You can impose simplicity by reducing complex elements to simpler forms.

For example, a detailed diagram of the human circulatory system would show the major blood vessels and organs. In a telescopic view the vessels are reduced to mere lines, and organs are reduced to simple geometric figures (as in the case of lungs and heart above). The purpose of reducing these elements to the barest outlines is that they are easily visualized and remembered.

There is no single "correct" way of choosing the elements that will be the outline or of picking the order of adding details. You will have to make these decisions with each new case. Nevertheless, organizing the layers is the most important step in the process—do it carefully. You will be learning the material as you plan your attack.

Maps, photographs, and charts can usually be made far less bewildering simply by rearranging their elements into easily remembered patterns. In the next quarter hour or so, you can learn the campus map shown in Figure 5.6 well enough to name the buildings and to give directions from any building to any other without looking at the map. This example gathers all the basic techniques we've used to date. Let yourself be led through this case—you can treat another map unassisted (in an exercise) at the end of the chapter.

The first step is to reduce the original map to an outline and layers of detail that can be remembered. This process is illustrated in Figures 5.7 through 5.9. Follow the reduction so that you will be able to sketch Figure 5.9 as follows:

1. Remember the outline in Figure 5.7.
2. Remember the first level of detail—the sectioning shown in Figure 5.8. (This may also be seen as two equal levels

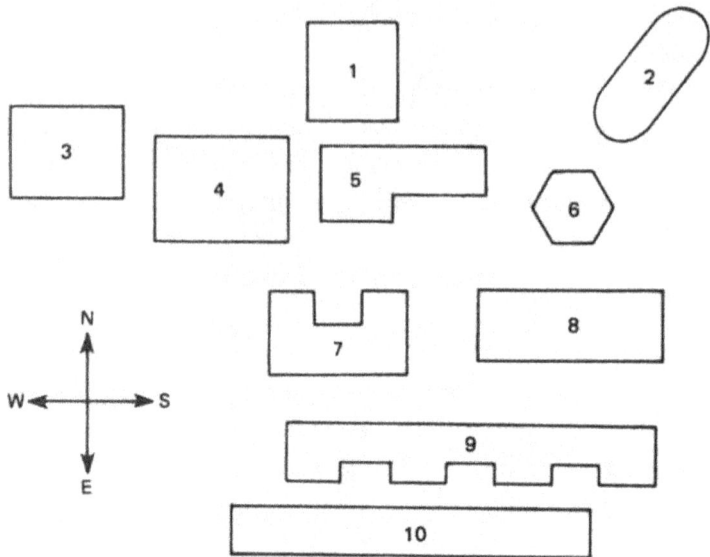

FIGURE 5.6

of detail, one for buildings 3 through 6 and another for buildings 7 through 10.)

3. Remember the second level of detail—the placement of the odd buildings 1 and 2 in Figure 5.9.

Check that you can reconstruct Figure 5.9 from memory. Now choose a substitute image to remind you of each building name:

1. The *Student Activities* building is represented by a mug of beer.
2. The *Gym* building is represented by a basketball.
3. The *Education* building is represented by chalk.
4. The *Administration* building is represented by the university president in long robes.

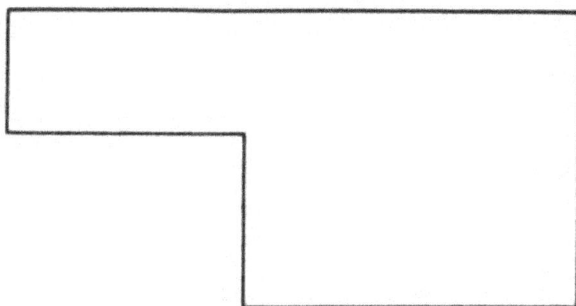

FIGURE 5.7

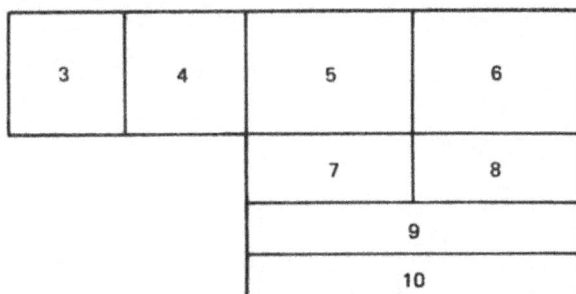

FIGURE 5.8

5. The *Law* building is represented by a judge's gavel (a more dynamic image than scales of justice).
6. The *Business* building is represented by a dollar bill.
7. The *Library* is represented by a book.
8. The *Theater* is represented by a mask of comedy.
9. The *Science* building is represented by a human-sized laboratory rat.
10. The *Dormitory* is represented by a bed.

Make vivid associations and be sure that you can identify each building name from the images in Figure 5.10.

Finally, link the images together with an absurd memory

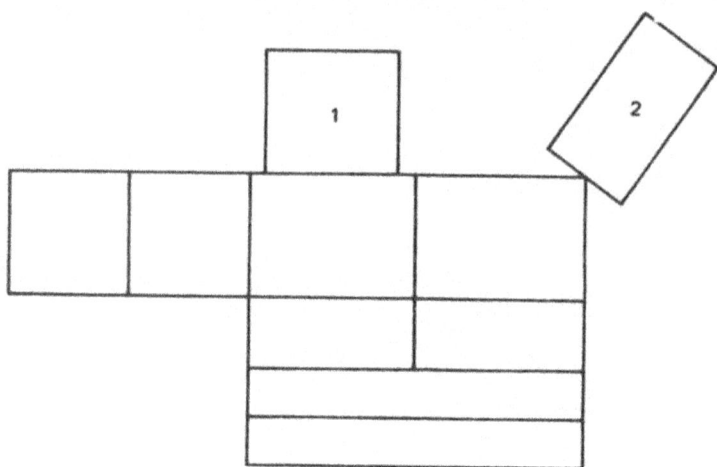

FIGURE 5.9

chain (the only new element here is that this is a *branched list*). Begin with *chalk* on the left, and imagine that the chalk writes on the president's clothes. This enrages the president, who seizes the gavel and smashes the dollar bill (to the right) and the book (below). The librarian is so upset that she disguises herself with the mask (to her right) and rides away on the giant rat (below her). The rat runs to the dormitory and goes to bed. As an afterthought, we remember the placement of the beer and the basketball by imagining beer dripping on the gavel below and a dollar bill growing into the basketball. Look at Figure 5.10 and visualize the nonsense clearly.

When you've completed these steps, cover the diagrams and answer these questions:

1. Which building is farthest west on campus? Farthest south? Farthest east?

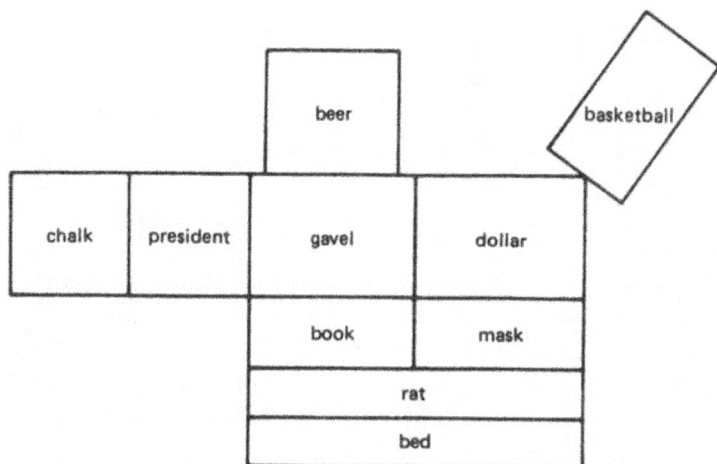

FIGURE 5.10

2. Which building is immediately east of the Education building?
3. In what direction should you go from the Administration building to reach the Law building?
4. In what direction should you go from the Law building to reach the Library? To reach the Business building? To reach the Student Activities building?
5. In what direction should you go from the Law building to reach the Science building?
6. In what direction should you go from the Theater to reach the Library? To reach the Business building?

SUMMARY

Telescoping: Telescoping is a technique whereby you first learn a broad outline, followed by successive layers of details.

Reduction process: Identify elements that seem most significant, and reduce these to a simple visualizable pattern. This is your outline. Memorize it. If you cannot decide which elements are "most significant," choose a few arbitrary elements. Your outline should be easy to visualize and recall, so do not begin with too many elements or overly complex geometric forms.

Details: Choose a level of details, preferably the most significant details, and remember these by linking them to the outline with vivid visual associations. Details may be any features you need to know, including labels, equations, and explanations. Repeat the process of adding layers of detail until the work is complete. Each layer should be strongly associated with the parts you have already treated.

EXERCISES

Your objective in the following exercises is to systematically apply the procedures of the above summary.

1. Figure 5.11 shows a nuclear reactor plant (old design). When the control rods are positioned as shown (not meshed with the fuel rods), nuclear reactions occur that heat water in the boiler. Steam drives the turbine and is then cooled to liquid water in the condenser, from which the water is pumped back to the boiler. The mechanical energy of the turbine is converted to electrical energy by the generator. Sketch the diagram from memory, describe the process, and identify the components.
2. A map of an industrial park is shown in Figure 5.12. Use telescoping to remember the map in sufficient detail to be able to tell, for any given building, the immediate neighboring buildings to the north, south, east, and west. (Reduce the map as shown in the text, and link the names of the buildings in a branched list.)

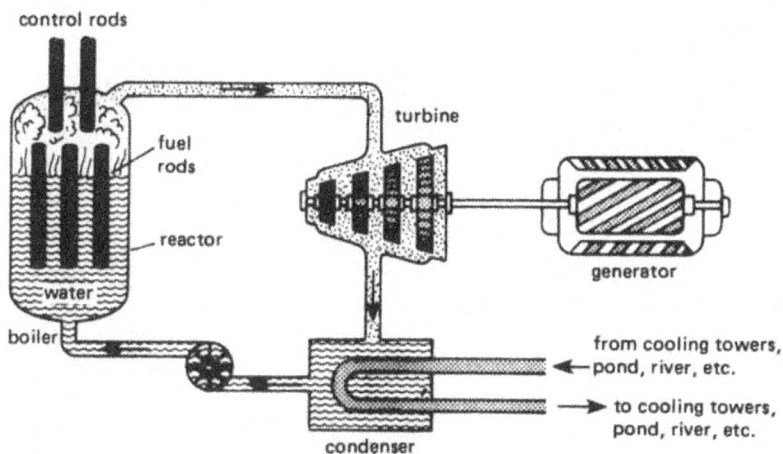

FIGURE 5.11

From *Energy: Resource, Slave, Pollutant,* Rouse and Smith. Copyright © by Macmillan Publishing Co., Inc. Reprinted by permission.

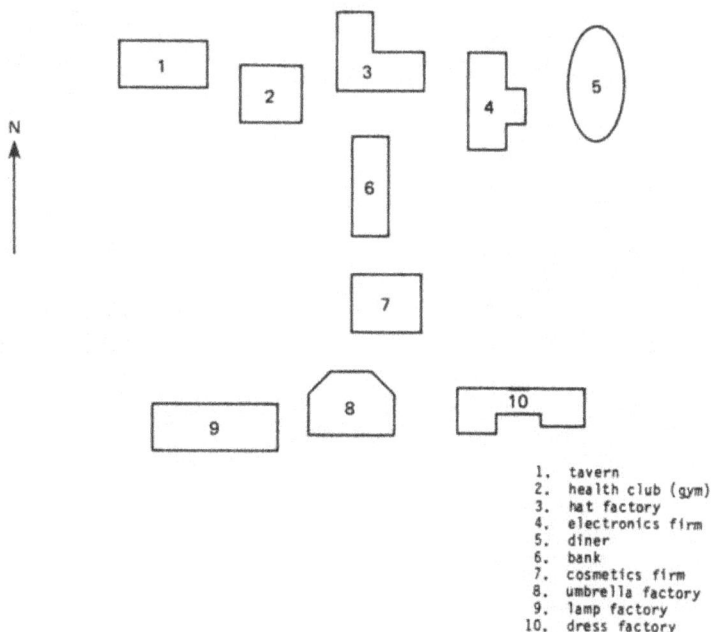

1. tavern
2. health club (gym)
3. hat factory
4. electronics firm
5. diner
6. bank
7. cosmetics firm
8. umbrella factory
9. lamp factory
10. dress factory

FIGURE 5.12

6

■

BETTER

LEARNING

■

Using the techniques for
best results

■

In a few short chapters you've performed electrifying feats of learning and remembering. The techniques you now know are fundamental for the techniques we have yet to treat. This is an appropriate place to consolidate and briefly discuss how to use techniques most advantageously.

FUNDAMENTALS

When I say that learning should use principles of organization, visualization, and association, it seems as prosaic as advice to carry an umbrella in threatening weather—sensible though obvious. But modern research indicates that these principles are fundamental, even essential, to learning.

The techniques you've been using are the vehicles of organization, visualization, and association. The telescopic approach is our principal technique for organizing information. It represents the hierarchical kind of thinking used by experts in diverse fields. Substitute imaging is our primary instrument of visualization, and memory chaining is the agent of association. Actually, visualization and association are not neatly separable, and imaging and chaining combine both.

There are several more central techniques to treat, but they are variations and combinations of the three you already know: telescoping, substitute imaging, and memory chaining.

TECHNIQUE VS. FRONTAL ATTACK

Techniques push you to approach material indirectly; the focus is more on how-to-do-it and less on the result. For example, in learning a detailed map you first concentrate on the outline instead of wallowing directly in the particulars. The details come later. Similarly, a pronounced difference between expert problem solvers and novices is that the experts concentrate on the solution ritual while novices stab directly for the answer.

The habit of making a frontal attack on material hinders good technique. It is natural to mount a direct assault, but battles conducted without strategy and tactics are wasteful even when they succeed. When you apply techniques and focus on the procedures, the results will follow.

No doubt people have many reasons to resist indirect approaches to learning. Some are concerned that techniques are games and not "true" learning. This is really an argument in favor of techniques, because game playing is a natural way of learning that is programmed into intelligent animals. A deeper but unspoken notion is that learning must be painful to be effective—a sad commentary on our educational experiences.

Perhaps the most mistaken concern is that the time spent in applying procedures is time away from learning. Be assured that you are learning as you apply techniques. This is true even if you don't succeed in completing the procedure. Your concentration and exposure to the material are greatest when you use techniques. Take the time to apply learning techniques—your time will not be wasted.

REAL LIFE

Alas, learning techniques are not a panacea. Techniques make learning easier and more effective, but not automatic.

"Real life" applications don't always follow clear blueprints. Sometimes you will encounter material that is fuzzier or more tortured than any presented in this book. Do not panic. Remember that you can always resort to your old methods, but you probably won't need to. As your experience grows, you can be more flexible and adapt the techniques to unusual cases.

Techniques do not replace good sense. It takes alertness—a "mental set"—to be ready to apply techniques. Simple, routine exchanges of information rarely warrant such intense concentration (except for practice). Life can become clumsy indeed for people trying to use techniques indiscriminately.

ON STUDY

Review and rest are important factors in effective study. Here are some guidelines to get the best results from review and rest.

Our techniques show that the human memory is much

stronger than people imagine. It is a curious paradox that memory is also less reliable and less accurate than the public believes. We fill gaps in our knowledge with imagination, so that the facts become distorted. Worse, we suffer from a flood of forgetting after study; an 80 percent loss of recall can occur in twenty-four hours. You've noticed that your memory is much more persistent when you use techniques, but some loss is inevitable.

Frequent reviews halt these memory distortions and decay. A good program of review is to rehearse the material at intervals of five to ten minutes, one day, one week, one month, and six months after the initial learning. Learning is then virtually permanent. The review sessions should take only a few minutes for each day of initial learning.

Study is also more effective with frequent rest breaks of five to ten minutes. Two factors help to make breaks useful: (1) We tend to remember best the first and last items in a study sequence, and breaks introduce more "first" and "last" items. (2) We remember more about five to ten minutes after studying than we do immediately after. A rest allows this consolidation to take place.

The optimum duration of a study period depends in part on the material. The longest periods should be given to conceptual material and the shortest to routine memory tasks. Most study periods should be under an hour and over fifteen minutes before resting. Then you can consolidate with few moments of review before continuing to the next study period.

PART

III

GENERAL
APPLICATIONS

The next four chapters apply the
techniques to subjects of wide
interest: vocabulary, languages,
terminology, readings, and
note taking.

7

■

VOCABULARY, LANGUAGES, TERMINOLOGY

■

Substitute imagery for learning vocabulary, terminology, and foreign languages

■

When memory giant Sheresheveskii took to the stage, audiences often challenged him to remember nonsensical words and phrases. Because of his learning "handicap," he was forced to convert the sounds into images. The technique he developed was to associate meaningful images with many sounds. This was so effective that, fifteen years after a single hearing of poetry in a foreign language, he was able to recall and pronounce it perfectly.

Of course, Sheresheveskii's approach required long, intense practice to develop a repertoire of symbols for every possible sound. For our purposes, this is more effort than it is worth—there are at least forty basic sounds in English. You can speed your learning of vocabulary and terminology severalfold with a much less demanding modification of his technique.

SOUNDS AND IMAGES

Perhaps the simplest way to remember unfamiliar words is to create substitute images that remind you of the sound of the original word. For example, the word *egregious* (meaning outstandingly bad) might be converted to *egg reach us*, which can be visualized. You can reconstruct the original sound with a bit of concentration.

Most often, the substitution sounds even less like the original: *tort* (a legal wrong subject to a civil suit) can be replaced by *tart*, and *pelf* (meaning ill-gotten wealth) can be changed to *elf*. Almost any fragments of the original sounds will serve as cues. Again, the most crucial step is forming a vivid image; this is far more important than worrying how closely the substitute sound matches the original.

In many cases it helps to use substitute words that rhyme with the original words. This shifts your attention to word endings, and it may be easier to find substitutes for these. Examples: *ouch* for *avouch* and *annoyed* for *sphenoid*.

Bear in mind that forming a substitute image is part of the learning process. The time you spend creating the substitutes is not wasted. Even when the substitute seems feeble, the effort and attention you devote to the original word make a bold impression on your memory. The technique does not relieve you of the need to concentrate on the word, but it makes your efforts more productive.

Three elements are involved when you learn an unfamiliar word: sound, meaning, and spelling. In most languages it is not difficult to spell a word when it is pronounced. Of course, there are many exceptions that trip weak spellers like me, but it is still good technique to concentrate first on sound and meaning and then to practice spelling separately.

You can link sound with meaning simply by extending your creative visualization process. For example, since *pelf* means dishonestly acquired wealth, you might visualize an elf running away with stolen money. The whole process is relatively easy to perform and can speed your learning rate for vocabulary and terminology severalfold.

APPLICATION: ENGLISH VOCABULARY

Use substitute imagery to learn the following list of vocabulary words. Treat three or four words at a time, and then review them just once before proceeding. Take your time. Even if you spend a minute or two devising a substitute image, you will be learning much faster and remembering much longer than you can by rote. Test yourself by recalling the meaning from the word and vice versa.

Word	Meaning	Suggested Imagery
egregious	outstandingly bad	*egg reach us*
defalcate	embezzle or misuse funds	*the fall cake* (Picture a cake falling apart, revealing embezzled money inside.)
mountebank	charlatan; con artist	Create your own vivid image for *mountebank*. Link this image to the meaning.
misogamy	hatred of marriage	*massage me*
hegira	flight from danger	Choose your own.
philatelist	stamp collector	*Phil ate the list*
avouch	to affirm: I will *avouch* the lawyer's integrity	Continue on your own.
panegyric	formal or public praise	Your choice.

Word	Meaning	Suggested Imagery
pelf	dishonestly acquired wealth	Your choice.
threnody	a song of lament; a dirge	Your choice.
tort	a legal wrong subject to civil action	Your choice.

APPLICATION: FRENCH VOCABULARY

Some French nouns are given below in phonetic form (without articles), together with their English translations. Use the procedures of this chapter to learn the list. Test yourself by recalling the English from the French and vice versa.

English	Phonetic French	Suggested Imagery
stomach	vahntr	*vendor* (Imagine a vendor with a huge stomach.)
road	root	Choose your own image.
bed	lee	*leaf*
world	mohnd	Your choice.
hunter	shah-SUHR	*chaser* (one who chases) or *masseur*
cakes	gah-TOH	Your choice.
basket	pah-N'YEH	Your choice.

Whole phrases may also be treated by the substitute image technique. The phrase *comment allez-vous (how are you)* might be stretched to *come and tally you,* and a bizarre scene may be imagined to link this sound to its meaning.

APPLICATION: TERMINOLOGY

Specialists in every field have their own language. Indeed, you can learn technical terms with the same approach you used for unfamiliar or foreign vocabulary words. The word *tort,* for instance, is a legal term that was included in our English vocabulary exercise.

A slightly different problem arises when you label bones or name computer components. Here you need to identify something rather than to define it. The approach is simple enough; associate the substitute image with the thing it represents.

You can use the technique to learn parts of the skull shown in Figure 7.1. The most far-fetched and silly substitutions will work when they are vivid and visual. For example, to recall the *parietal* bone you can substitute *pear tail* and imagine a pear with a tail growing out of that part of the head. Some other substitutes can be even stranger. Look at the list of bones and substitute images below.

Bone	Substitute Image
parietal	*pear tail*
coronal suture	Someone suggested *core suit* to prompt the recall of both words; the image is an apple core dressed in a suit. Entirely different images arise if you know that *coronal* refers to a crown and *suture* is a stitch.
frontal	This appears so easy that you are likely to forget it due to insufficient visualization. Imagine headlights on this bone; you will not forget that it relates to the "front."
sphenoid	Try your own.
temporal	Try your own.
mastoid process	Try your own.
zygoma	Here is an imaginative one. I visualize "Brand Z" chewing gum. That is, Z-*gum*. An alternative is *sigh coma*. I leave the imagery to you.
mandible	Try your own.
mental foramen	*Foramen* applies to a small hole in the bone. Try your own images.

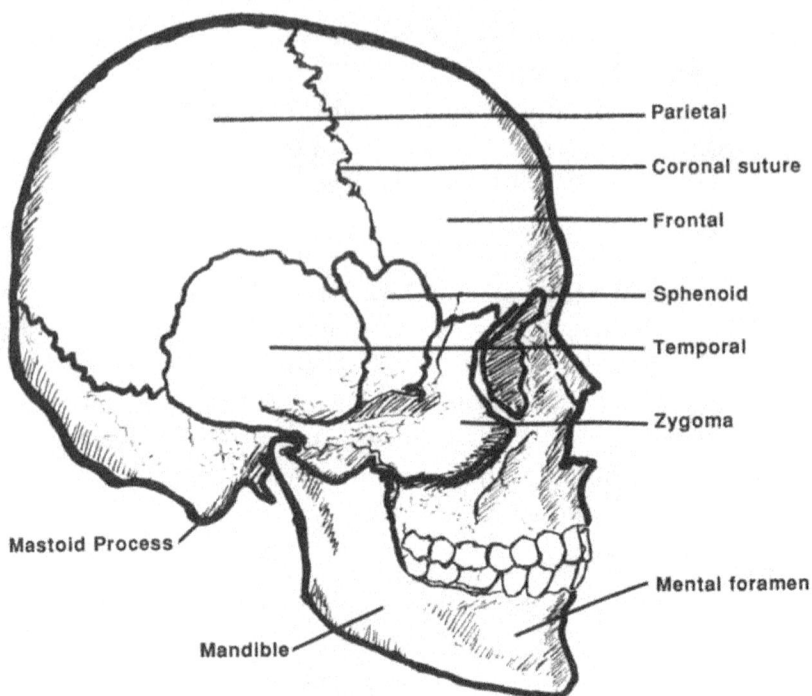

FIGURE 7.1

EXERCISE

Memorize the facial bones labeled on the right side of the diagram. Refer to the list above for suggestions and comments. Treat three or four items at a time, and then review them just once. When you are finished, cover the labels and repeat the names in any order.

8

■

MAPPING
THOUGHTS

■

A telescopic approach for
summarizing facts and ideas

■

The name of your first love or a mention of your hometown can stir a storm of memories. Other words, phrases, and images remind you of facts and ideas. It is not surprising that such key words play an important role in recalling readings, lectures, and films, particularly when combined with other techniques. These applications are treated in later chapters. This chapter shows how to choose key words and arrange them in maps—thought maps that enable you to retrieve ideas and facts.

CHOOSING KEY WORDS OR IMAGES

It takes attention and effort to summarize a thought with key words. In fact, your efforts at choosing key words are an important part of the learning process.

For example, the following sentence is taken from an article about the history of Chief Justice Burger's court:

Warren E. Burger's tenure as Chief Justice of the Supreme Court is characterized by decisions that are narrowly constructed technical compromises that avoid sweeping legal principles.

You want to select key words—the fewer, the better—that will remind you of the central idea. Certainly this process is subjective, and there are many possible choices. I prefer the key word *narrow* to remind me that technical compromises are characteristics of the Burger court. Other choices are *sweeping legal principles* or (better) *sweeping*; these work even though they suggest the opposite of the "narrow" idea. You can easily remember that the original idea is the antithesis of your key word. *Burger* or *Supreme Court* are poor choices in this context because these are the subjects of an entire article and therefore not sufficiently specific to unlock the "narrow" idea.

Key images are often preferable to key words. For the previous example, an image of a narrow hamburger is a vivid reminder of narrow legal decisions by the Burger court. It is convenient to understand that the term key word includes key images as well.

EXERCISE

Only rarely do you need to remember ideas sentence by sentence. As an exercise, however, it is worthwhile to write key words for each of the six sentences in the abstract below. Choose key words that will remind you of the basic idea or fact in each sentence.

Abstract: Components of Memory
(1) Recent research in human memory suggests that memory functions can be separated into three components. (2) The first is sensory memory, with which we momentarily grasp sights and sounds all around us. (3) These sensory impressions last less than one second before they fade away. (4) The second component of

memory, short-term memory, is associated with consciousness; it holds the thought-of-the-moment. (5) Finally, long-term memory is the component that stores huge amounts of information more or less permanently. (6) We become conscious of sensory memories and stored long-term memories only when they are moved into short-term memory, where they can be held under continual attention.

Use your list of key words to see how much you can remember about each of the original statements. Of course, you do not need to repeat the original statement verbatim. Most likely you will require one review to secure all the statements in this dense paragraph.

THOUGHT MAPS

Key words are more effective when they are arranged in maps. Maps are constructed with a telescopic approach, whereby you first find a central idea (the *core point*) and then decorate it with key words for subordinate ideas and facts.

The paragraph of the last exercise can serve as an example. Perhaps the most central statement is that there are three components to memory; a natural key word is *three*. The names of these components can be seen as subordinate to this. We sketch this situation in the form of a map.

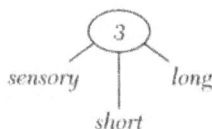

Adding further details introduces the functions and features of the components:

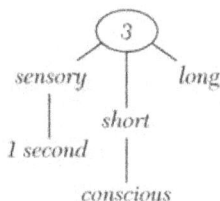

59

These maps of key words are *thought maps* (some authors use the term *mind map*). Notice how easily you can remember the abstract in thought-map form as compared with the linear sequence of key words you used in the last exercise.

You may have noticed that my thought map does not contain all the information it might. For instance, the information in sentence 6, indicating that we can be aware of a memory only if it is moved into short term, is not represented explicitly. The reason is that I expect to remember the idea simply by seeing the key word *conscious* in context.

Most written material is filled with small details that support the central points and add color and clarity to the message. Usually it is quite unimportant to remember such minutiae. Using a telescopic approach, you can construct a thought map to include a little or a lot of detail. We can say that our thought-map example includes details to the "second level," although this terminology is rather loose, since some items might be treated in more layers of detail than others.

FINDING CORE POINTS

A thought map is like a box full of related ideas and facts. There is one central point, the core point, that is used as a label and summarizes the contents of the box. The most effective way to boost reading comprehension is to find these core points.

The search is easier when you recognize that the core point is the most *general* idea in a thought map. It summarizes the broad idea, but not the details, of the map. In fact, the core point is not always the most informative point in the map. Rather, it is the most encompassing label for the box of ideas; it is the umbrella statement that covers the other statements in the thought map.

The main distinction you must make is between *general* and *specific* (or detailed) statements. In the following "paragraphs" the sentences are out of order. In each one, find the most general idea in the group. Check that each of the other sentences either elaborates, explains, or gives details about the sentence you choose.

EXERCISE

Choose the most general statement from the following scrambled paragraphs. Answers are given below.

Paragraph 1

1. Shade trees around the home cut down on light for indoor plants.
2. The direction a window faces determines the quality of light coming through it.
3. Plant growth depends on how much natural light is available.
4. A house next door can also block light.

Paragraph 2

1. Certainly, the call to "come here" should be obeyed.
2. A dog's welfare depends on its having been taught some basic discipline.
3. Training your pet to walk on a leash is important.
4. It does not break the spirit of a dog to obey voice commands.

Paragraph 3

1. A look into the near future will provide you with tasks to accomplish.
2. Make a priority list of those tasks to be accomplished today.
3. A few basic steps can help you to manage your time.
4. Allocate hours or minutes to each task on the list.
5. Then put the day's schedule on your calendar and follow it.

ANSWERS

Paragraph 1

1. Shade trees are specific agents that reduce the light.
2. Window direction is a specific factor affecting the quality of light.
3. This is the most general statement. All others are specifics regarding "how much natural light is available."
4. A house next door is a specific agent that reduces light.

61

Paragraph 2

1. Obeying the call to "come here" is a specific part of dog discipline.
2. This is the most general statement. All others mention specific disciplines.
3. Walking on a leash is a specific discipline.
4. This sentence is easily mistaken as the most general, but when you compare this with sentence 2, you see that voice commands are part of basic discipline.

Paragraph 3

1. This sentence is often mistaken as the most general. Comparison with sentence 3, however, shows that collecting tasks is just a specific step in managing your time.
2. Making a priority list is a specific step in managing your time.
3. This is the most general statement.
4. Allocating time to tasks is a specific step in managing your time.
5. Making a schedule is another specific step in managing your time.

As you look for core points, it helps to know that the central idea in a paragraph is in either the first or last sentence in about 80 percent of cases. As a consequence, a core point is most likely to come from these sentences. (The term *topic sentence* is avoided here because core points are more general—core points can extend beyond a single paragraph, and topic sentences cannot.)

Where are the central ideas of the other 20 percent of all paragraphs? They may be anywhere in the paragraph. In some cases the central idea is not stated, and you are left to infer your own.

MAP STRUCTURE

It is useful practice to sketch thought maps for a few paragraphs. Ovals are used to represent core points, and circles represent supporting points. As an example, examine the map we construct for the following paragraph:

(1) A few basic steps can help you to manage your time. (2) First, a look into the near future will provide you with tasks to accomplish. (3) Next, make a priority list of those tasks to be accomplished today. (4) Allocate hours or minutes to each task on the list. (5) Then put the day's schedule on your calendar and follow it.

The corresponding thought map is shown in Figure 8.1. Notice that it shows the direct relation between points 3 and 4.

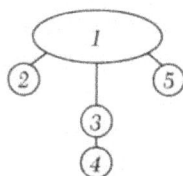

FIGURE 8.1

EXERCISE

Find the core point in the paragraph below using the criteria of (1) generality and (2) sentence placement. Sketch a thought map using sentence numbers as labels.

(1) Male bodybuilders use exercise and diet to develop special qualities. (2) Huge muscle size or "bulk" is the most obvious attribute. (3) But equally important is the sharp definition of the muscles that makes them stand out like steel cables under the skin. (4) Good definition requires fat-free musculature to reveal the fine lines. (5) More subtle, but perhaps most coveted, is symmetry, where the body has a graceful, balanced shape.

Now key words, core points, and mapping can be put together again. See Figure 8.2 for one possibility for the thought map of the time-management example.

FIGURE 8.2

EXERCISE

Sketch a thought map of the bodybuilding paragraph with key words rather than numbers. (Your number map should look like the number map for the time-management example.)

So far we used thought maps for single paragraphs. This is too limiting. Thought maps embrace ideas and facts that transcend paragraphs and sentences. Often you can use just one map for a section of many paragraphs. Occasionally you may want to map a single informative sentence.

It is acceptable, even desirable, to create thought maps with some imaginative forms. However, try to make them easy to visualize. A few variations are shown in Figure 8.3.

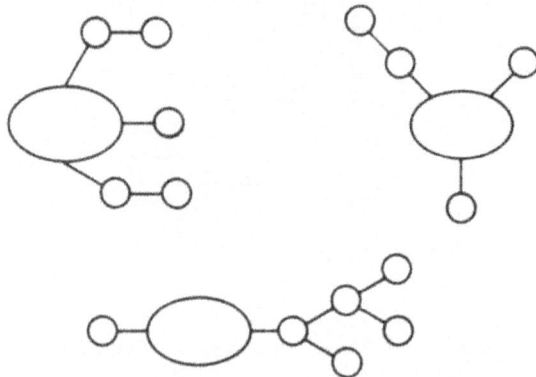

FIGURE 8.3

Thought maps are instruments of telescopic and visual thinking. They are the basis for reading and note-taking techniques described in later chapters. And maps are graphics of mental organization—like words, you can think with them without writing them down.

SUMMARY

Choosing key words and images: Choose key words or key images that seem best to remind you of an idea or fact. The fewer key words for each idea, the better. Feel free to choose key words or images that express the antithesis of an idea—you will recognize it as such.

Finding core points: A core point is the most *general idea in a thought map; other points in the map are specifics* relating to the core. Look for general encompassing core points.

Core points can often be found among the first or last sentences of paragraphs.

Constructing thought maps: (1) Write key words or images for the core point of the map; (2) Attach key words for a first level of subordinate information to the core point; (3) Continue the process of adding key words for successive layers of detail to the key words of the preceding level. Stop when you have reached a satisfactory level of detail.

EXERCISE

Follow the steps in the summary to devise a single thought map for each of the following short articles. Draw the map only to about a second level of detail, and see that you can recall the basic information from the map.

Remove Scratch Marks on Glass

Are scratches detracting from your windows, sliding glass doors, or watch face? You can repair these and other glass scratches simply with household products.

An ordinary cleansing powder like Bon Ami can be used as a buffing powder. Of course, you can buy commercial buffing powders from many paint and glass stores.

The powder should be applied with a damp cloth or towel and rubbed well. A precaution: tempered glass may shatter from the heat of machine buffing. We recommend hand buffing for this reason.

Scratches may be too deep for buffing if you can feel them with your fingernail. You may still remove the scratches with much rubbing, but a wavy effect can develop. Of course, they may be preferable to scratches.

Touch, Taste, and the Desire to Eat

How important is cool creaminess to the appeal of ice cream, juicy chewiness to the allure of a steak, or crunchiness to the craving for an apple? Studies of pigeons and rats have recently shown that the feel of food in the mouth is a more important factor in the desire to eat than taste is.

Traditionally, we think of taste as the most significant oral element in eating. But Dr. H. Philip Zeigler, an animal-behavior researcher from New York's Hunter College, decided to investigate how the *feel* of food is related to appetite.

To do this, he severed the nerves that provide tactile sensation in pigeons and rats, leaving alone their ability to taste. Zeigler observed that in both species this caused a sudden and dramatic drop in the amount of time spent eating. Since the animals were still able to eat, Zeigler concluded that they did not want to eat—their appetites simply died.

A striking aspect of Zeigler's discovery was that the loss of interest in eating occurred immediately after the mouth's tactile nerves were severed. The animals did not have to eat first for loss of appetite to take place.

During several weeks of abstaining almost entirely from food, the weights of the pigeons and rats fell by over 20 percent. Eventually many of them resumed their normal feeding patterns, but they never ate in sufficient quantity to regain normal adult weight.

In a separate experiment using another test group, Zeigler severed the nerves that transmit *taste* perception to the brain. In contrast, he found the loss of feeding activity to be minimal and transient. His conclusion: the inability to feel food diminishes, specifically and dramatically, the desire to eat, whereas the inability to taste food does not.

The imagination jumps to the notion that this could lead to a remedy that millions of overeaters are seeking. Zeigler, however, dismisses the feasibility of severing nerves in people—the complexity of nerve structures would offer too many opportunities for surgical disaster. He does speculate, though, that elimination of oral touch sensation, and hence appetite, may be possible by altering the action of certain nerve-signal chemicals. Development of this form of treatment has not even been attempted, and Zeigler speculates it would take at least ten years of intensive research. (Michael L. Zoler, *Science Digest*.)

Development of Language and Speech

Normal children have, at birth, the potential to walk and to talk, although as babies they can do neither. They are genetically endowed with the appropriate neurophysical systems, but time is needed for these systems to develop and mature. The brain is approximately 40 percent of the size it will attain by adulthood; the more peripheral areas, the vocal tract and the legs, await the anatomical change and the development of motor-sensory associations appropriate to talking and walking. At 6 months, children sit up and *babble* in meaningless vocal play. By the arrival of the first birthday, they may have started to walk and to name things. By the second birthday, they may be putting two words together for rudimentary telegraphic sentences, and by the fourth, they will have mastered the essential rules of the language of their elders. The rapidity and apparent ease with which children learn language is a phenomenon of childhood and can never be repeated with such ease by adults. Many adults learn new languages, especially those who already know several languages, but the time most conducive to learning languages is before puberty. Wilder Penfield, the Canadian neurophysiologist, put the cut-off at about 15. The best time for learning language, however, is during the first 4 years.

What children universally accomplish with spontaneity and speed, psychologists, linguists, and speech scientists have laboriously analyzed with only moderate success. The question they ask is How do children acquire language? Theorists on this subject can be generally divided into two groups. One group of theorists analyzes language development in terms of learning principles. The other group analyzes language development in terms of an innate propensity for language. Perhaps the most currently popular view is that only the details or individual items of a particular language are learned, while the structural and creative underpinnings universal to all languages are inherited. (Gloria J. Borden and Katherine S. Harris, *Speech Science Primer*.)

9

■

READING

■

Reading with greater
comprehension and recall

■

Jane S., a prominent state official, prepares for news conferences by reading reports with agonizing intensity. Her desk is littered with coffee cups and cigarette butts as her eyes burn down each page—line by line, fact after fact. She is reading to remember.

Jane's approach is painfully familiar to most of us. When the information is important, we fear that reading less carefully will cause us to miss important points. We are sure we will remember less with a faster, less intense reading. Fortunately, these concerns are misguided—there is a better way.

Not every reading needs to be remembered in detail. Usually, it is sufficient to remember only the broadest topic outlines. Of course, you need to remember details when you are being tested, when you present the material to others, or when the particulars are important for the routine conduct of your business or profession. In other cases it makes more sense simply to skim and file the information with no attempt to remember it.

You recognize these extreme goals in reading: reading to remember and reading for a general idea. We would like to remember everything we read, but the reality is that we must invest time and effort to increase both original learning and recall. It is more efficient to use high-speed techniques of previewing and skimming for general content and a telescopic approach for graphic recall.

THE FORMAT OF BOOKS, REPORTS, AND ARTICLES

The time you spend in organizing reading material is not wasted. Indeed, organizing can be the most useful step in the learning process, especially for complex or dense material. The first step in this organization is to be clearly aware of the format of books, reports, and articles.

Textbooks generally have a format of chapters, sections, and paragraphs (see Figure 9.1). Of course, there are variations on this theme. Often the chapters are themselves organized into broader subject headings; a physics test may include the headings "Mechanics," "Heat," "Waves," and so on, each of which comprise several chapters. Another variation has sections subdivided into subsections; an art text may have

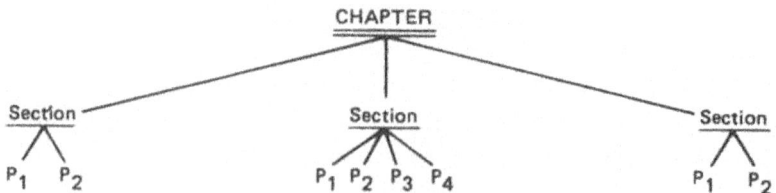

FIGURE 9.1

70

a section entitled "The Renaissance Period" that is further divided into the subsections "Early Renaissance" and "Late Renaissance."

Long reports generally have formats similar to books, but a good report often has the additional virtue of having a succinct abstract and a conclusion or summary. Take advantage of these attributes and read the abstract and the conclusion or summary first.

Articles and short reports usually have a format similar to a single chapter in a textbook. Often, especially in shorter articles, the section captions are omitted, and the copy appears as an unbroken list of paragraphs. In these cases you can gain an advantage by imposing your own section headings.

Review the organization of a book or long article before you read it. Examine any table of contents, section headings, and abstract or summary to get some idea of where the text is going and how it will get there.

READING FOR A GENERAL IDEA

The fastest reading techniques exploit the fact that you can catch the overall meaning in readings without reading every word. This is a reasonable approach to avoiding unnecessary reading. Many people claim reading rates well above 1,000 words per minute, although the physiological limit seems to be less than 800 words per minute. These readers are not lying—they are reading well without actually seeing all the words.

People expect too much from rapid-reading techniques because of publicity about speed reading. The reading rates of University of Michigan professors who were tested averaged 300 words per minute. These are highly intelligent professionals with lifelong practice in taking ideas and information from the printed page—but 300 words per minute is seen as deficient according to speed-reading advocates. More likely, the deficiency lies in how success in reading is being assessed. If you read 1,000 words per minute at 70 percent comprehension, do you learn more than reading 300 words per minute at 100 percent comprehension? The numbers suggest that in the first case you learn 700 words per minute and only 300 words per minute in the second. The trouble is that you may need to know that missing 30 percent to remove a gall bladder, file a legal brief, or design a bridge.

You can get a general idea of long and difficult readings by *previewing:* read the first two paragraphs, then read only the first sentence of the following paragraphs, and read the last two paragraphs. Also read all topic and section headings.

Previewing is suitable for a quick overview of heavy, long readings such as textbook chapters and for long articles and reports. It can increase your reading rate five- or tenfold, with as much as 50 percent comprehension. You can always decide whether you want a closer reading.

Articles usually orient the reader within the first two paragraphs and summarize in the last two. Most important, a majority of core points are given in the first sentences of paragraphs. These sentences, together with topic and section headings, reveal much of the basic content.

Another technique for rapid reading is *skimming*. It is slower but more thorough than previewing. And, of course, it is faster than standard reading. Authorities in rapid reading usually refer to skimming as picking out only a few key words from every line. Skimming is used here as a search—a search for core points.

You found core points for thought maps by looking for general, inclusive points—usually from among the beginnings or ends of paragraphs. Skimming, for our purposes, is making this search while only glancing at the subordinate facts, details, supporting statements, and specifics of all kinds.

Skimming focuses on central points, but peripheral information rubs off in the search. This technique is valuable, not only for general ideas, but as a preliminary step in reading to remember.

Standard reading is what most of us do when there is no need to rush or memorize. Previewing and skimming have uses, as does the heavy artillery of reading to remember, but these should be reserved for when they are needed. Contrary to the opinion of some advocates of speed reading, there is no shame in just reading.

READING TO REMEMBER

Reading and remembering difficult material is always hard study, but it can be made easier with a telescopic approach. The basic idea is to see the structure of the reading in layers: the overall format, core points, first level of specifics, and so on. And usually each layer is treated in a separate pass through the material. The information is recorded in thought maps, which are easily memorized.

In most of what follows I will have you focus on reading and mapping for higher levels of detail—as if you were preparing for a test or presentation. It will then be easy to relax your approach for less demanding cases.

The first "reading" should be a mere skim of a section. Try to answer only one question: in the broadest terms, what are the most central ideas or facts in this section? Some sections may encompass only one fundamental idea, others may include several. Surprisingly, sections often contain no truly basic points. This is frequently true of introductory sections that orient the reader to the topic.

The central points are usually easy to find in clearly written material, but texts and reports can be notoriously opaque. The burden then falls to you to select core points, and often there are several alternative choices, some giving better organization than others. In such cases, it is worth taking a few moments to decide on a set of core points that appear to best reflect the structure of the information.

When you have found the central points (if any) in a section, write key words or images for each. These will serve as the cores of thought maps.

Now reread the section just closely enough to identify a first level of detail, and include key words for these details on the thought maps. Continue rereading and adding to the maps until you attain the desired level of detail. Bear in mind that you do not need to include every nuance on the thought map. Your natural memory will fish up associated points pertaining to the recorded key words and images. When you finish the first section, repeat the process for succeeding sections.

You want to be flexible with this procedure. Often, subordinate points are so clearly bristling from a core point that it would be silly to wait for a later pass to include them. In other cases, only an occasional detail needs to be attached to a point to avoid another reading. But whenever things are difficult or cloudy, it helps to leave specifics for another pass.

The result of the full procedure is a set of thought maps. These are easily memorized as they were recorded, in a layered sequence. The cores of thought maps are linked in a memory chain, then a first level of specifics is associated with each core, etc. For the present, it will be enough to record the maps. You are experienced in remembering maps from chapter 5.

Does it take more time to execute repeated readings instead of reading very closely just once? No, not for equivalent results. There are clear benefits of organization and internal association in using this iterative technique (as with all telescopic approaches). Moreover, the readings are rapid because the reader focuses on one level at a time with a minimum of regression, a major cause of slow reading.

DOING LESS

Reading to remember is a powerful but demanding collection of techniques. I recommend that you first become comfortable with the full procedure, although you can usually have excellent reading recall with much less effort.

You may, for example, read for the central points only (the cores of the maps). As you read, you can link these points without writing any notes. An occasional important detail can be linked mentally with the core points. Even this simplified version of the full approach greatly improves a reader's ability to remember. I find that I use this lean approach for most of my reading to remember.

Many readers underline or highlight readings. These approaches may be regarded as substitutes for sketching thought maps. If highlighting is your preference, try not to highlight too much; students' textbooks are sometimes 70 percent or more highlighted—a sure waste of effort. Highlight only material that you would otherwise summarize on a thought map. Several people have reported that highlighting in two colors, one for core points and one for details, helped their reading recall.

SUMMARY

Reading for a general idea: Previewing is used for long difficult readings. Read the first two paragraphs, the first sentence of the following paragraphs, and the last two paragraphs. Include all topic and section headings.

Skimming is searching for core points while only glancing at the subordinate points. Look especially for general, inclusive points from the beginnings or ends of paragraphs.

Reading to remember: This is a telescopic approach where the structure of the reading is seen in layers: format, core points, first-level specifics, etc. The information is recorded in thought maps.

Examine the formats of books, reports, and articles before reading. Look at any table of contents and at chapter and section headings. Read any abstract, conclusions, or summary first. Try to see where the text is going and how it will get there.

Reading and mapping: (1) Skim a section (or the equivalent) to find the central point(s). Record key words for each central point; these serve as cores for maps. (2) Repeatedly reread the section, adding a level of details to the thought maps with each reading. Stop when you have treated enough detail. Do not try to record every particular—the maps will remind you of more detail than you have recorded. (3) Repeat the second step for each section.

For most purposes, excellent reading recall is obtained with far fewer steps than the full procedure outlined above. For example, the second step may be eliminated entirely when fine details are unimportant.

EXERCISE

Apply the summary's reading and mapping instructions to the reading selection that follows or to any short, informative article that interests you. Construct thought maps to a second level of detail (where warranted), and check that you can reconstruct the basic information from the maps.

The Black Death

One-third of the people of the world dead, 36 percent of the universities closed, 50 percent of the clergy dead. Europe devastated in only three years. Towns deserted, farms lying idle, and gloom over the entire continent. This is the picture in 1351 at the end of the Black Death, the bubonic plague that swept from Asia throughout the civilized world in the great epidemic of the fourteenth century.

Bubonic plague is a disease spread primarily by fleas that usually live on rodents. The disease is spread among the rodents (often rats) by the fleas, and humans contract the disease from fleas, especially when the rat population decreases because of disease. The fleas then seek human hosts.

Actually, the bubonic plague of the fourteenth century had three different forms. The first, involving bubons, or boils, at the lymph nodes in the groin or armpits, is spread primarily by fleas. In the second form, in which pneumonia is involved with disease of the lungs, transmission can occur directly between human beings. The third form, involving the nervous system, is highly contagious and causes death within hours.

The first recorded instance of the plague occurred in the Near East in the eleventh century B.C. Apparently, there are regions of northern India and central Asia where the plague is continually latent. Worldwide epidemics have started there at least three times during the last 2,000 years.

The first great pandemic (an epidemic covering the civilized world) occurred in the sixth century A.D. Lasting fifty years, "Justinian's plague" involved the Roman world and certainly was one factor in the disintegration of the Roman Empire.

The latest pandemic started in the middle of the last century in China, reached Hong Kong by the start of this century, and then spread throughout the world from the Chinese ports. With an estimated 10 million deaths in India, the epidemic was most serious in Asia. With the concept of quarantine established in Europe by about 1720, the emphasis on sanitation and hospitalization during the last century, and improved urban sewage-disposal and rat-control systems, the epidemic did not seriously affect the western world. In more recent years, particularly with the use of antibiotics, bubonic plague has been well controlled with only 200 deaths per year over the last decade.

The great pandemic of the fourteenth century started in northern India. It is not known why the plague began its spread. Apparently, the rodent population that normally carries the disease was forced to migrate, because of food shortage, excessive rain, earthquakes, or other reasons.

The plague reached western Europe in 1347 and primary effects lasted for the next three years during which more than 30 million Europeans died, or a third of the population. Actually the epidemic followed the normal pattern and recurred over the next two centuries before finally subsiding, but the term "Black Death" usually refers to the first catastrophic three years.

While the plague undoubtedly was brought to Europe in several ways, historians often spotlight the primary source as the Tartar siege of the Crimean port of Kaffa in 1347. As so often happens in war, thousands of men were brought together in unsanitary conditions, in this case in a region infested by rats. The Tartars began dying by the thousands and finally dispersed.

Once the siege was lifted, ships immediately sailed for Genoa, Italy. When the ships reached Genoa, they were sent away and then carried the plague to Sicily, Spain, and northern Africa.

The chronology of the epidemic gives a picture of the plague fanning out from the Italy-Sicily region northward, westward, and eastward:

1348 N. Africa, Spain, France
1349 Austria, Hungary, Switzerland, Netherlands, northern Germany, England
1350 Scandinavia, Scotland, Ireland

The size of the catastrophe is emphasized by the death rates, which varied from one-eighth to two-thirds. Investigations of the death toll in Europe at that time are reported by W. Langer:

As reported by chroniclers of the time, the mortality figures were so incredibly high that modern scholars long regarded them with skepticism. Recent detailed and rigorously conducted analyses indicate, however, that many of the reports were substantially correct. It is now generally accepted that at least a quarter of the European population was wiped out in the first epidemic of 1348 through 1350, and that in the next fifty years the total mortality rose to more than a third of the population. The incidence of the disease and the mortality rate varied, of course, from place to place. Florence was reduced in population from 99,000 to 15,000; Hamburg apparently lost almost two-thirds of its inhabitants. (William L. Langer, *The Black Death*)

Langer further reports:

It is now estimated that the total population of England fell from about 3.8 million to 2.1 million in the period from 1348 to 1373. In France, where the loss of life was increased by the Hundred Years War, the fall in population was even more precipitate. In western and central Europe as a whole the mortality was so great that it took nearly two centuries for the population level of 1348 to be regained.

In many areas, the population did not return to its pre-plague level until 500 years later. The tragic extent of the epidemic was largely a result of the totally inadequate state of medical knowledge. The only treatments were bleeding, or the smelling or eating of aromatic herbs and unusual foods.

Because of the scarcity of carefully prepared histories of the fourteenth century, it is impossible to determine in detail the effects of the disaster. Clearly, the most profound aftermath was the deep impression of the epidemic left on the people. The disease often dragged its victims through days of intense suffering, accompanied by extensive vomiting and a pervading stench surrounding the victim. When the bubons broke, black blood was discharged and the patient often died lying in a pool of the liquid. With an average of two people per household affected, few individuals in Europe escaped without direct contact with the plague. (Polytechnic Institute of Brooklyn, *The Man-Made World*)

10

■

ON

NOTES

■

Note taking and studying
from notes

■

A "notebook check" was a ter-
rifying event. My teacher walked around the classroom and
leafed through the students' notebooks, each as elegant and
thick as a bible. I could hear my pulse as she approached my
desk and the sloppy, scant scribble in my notebook. At last
she was standing over me writing "unsatisfactory" everywhere
and lecturing that a sloppy notebook reflects a sloppy mind.

I accepted that judgment for decades, but now I believe
my sketchy notes were better for their purpose than the
glorious volumes my teachers adored. All notes are summaries of ideas and information; the style of your notes should
fit the functions you want them to serve. Some people might
want a detailed abstract, but you might prefer notes that are

personal reminders of material already learned, or you may simply need a permanent record of names, numbers, and other details.

NOTES AS ABSTRACTS

Notes can be rewrites of the original subject matter. These are abstracts that are literate, neat, and complete—they can be read by anyone.

Such notes include the infamous reviews of classic literature often read by schoolchildren in lieu of the originals. How this practice is despised by teachers! Nevertheless, when factual information—as distinct from an appreciation of literature— is being demanded from students, this is the student's best alternative. Condensation-type notes can serve as an outline for a telescopic approach. When you can obtain a condensation of any subject matter, it makes sense to review it first. For learning purposes, it is far better to read such notes than to write them.

Most people do strive to write ideal condensation-type notes and many, including my former classmates, succeed admirably. The problem is that it is very difficult to write extensive notes and learn at the same time.

Watch a busy note taker at a lecture; you can almost see the information passing into his ear, down his arm, and onto the paper without ever touching his brain. If learning could be ensured by simply recording information, shorthand would be an essential study skill.

TAKING NOTES

Of course, it is important to make permanent records of information that you cannot trust to memory or that is useless or burdensome to memorize. An effective note-taking format will help you keep such records without excessive transcription. In previous chapters you used thought maps to take notes from readings. Thought maps also work for most other vehicles of information, including lectures, presentations, and nonprint media.

The structure of thought maps assists learning and remembering. The core of each map is a central idea or fact represented by key words. (Listening or reading for central ideas demands close attention; it is a forced learning process.) Subordinate information radiates from the cores in a picturesque fashion, and the maps become more effective when they are embellished with sketches, designs, and coloring. Try these touches and see if they suit you. Keep the maps compact and visually simple—a liberal use of abbreviations will help.

Notes taken when listening and viewing are likely to be brief because time is limited by the rate of the presentation. Since more time is available when taking notes from printed matter, some readers will rewrite or highlight extensive passages. Resist this tedious practice. Certainly the process of writing information, together with hearing or seeing it, helps us to learn. This is particularly true of vocabulary, terminology, and the like. Facts and ideas, however, are learned more efficiently when they are summarized as succinctly as possible.

Your goal should be to learn and take notes simultaneously. This requires that you trust your ability to reconstruct the full information from thought maps. It helps to let your confidence evolve by first writing maps that are almost as complete as the notes you now take. You can gradually make them shorter by relying more on key words and less on exposition.

Most people proceed this way before they become adept at mapping.

Be aware that note taking is seldom a precision process. Not every core point is easily recognizable, with the subordinate points clearly organized around the core. This is the ideal, but all too often the importance of various points is not clear until later. Record any questionable points in a conventional form. When you review these notes you can reconstruct them in visual map form. Temporarily discard the map format whenever it doesn't seem to fit the information—mapping should assist and not restrict you.

STUDYING NOTES

Review your notes as soon as possible. This ensures that you will remember the meanings of your key words and terse personal messages. The review does not need to be a deep study. Simply check that you can reconstruct the information from the notes. Write short explanations for items that seem too cryptic. This is likely to be enough study for some subject matter.

When you study more difficult material, it helps to distill it with repeated reductions. You then have a layered view of the information, so that one level reminds you of the next in a cascade of associations—the telescopic approach. Memorization can be carried to any desired level by the procedures described below.

Information cast in thought maps is already reduced and easily remembered. Within each topic unit, say a chapter, the cores of the maps can be linked in a memory chain. This is enough to remember the basics. Many details are likely to be recalled from the cores after a simple review.

Complete maps can be memorized by treating them as

branched lists where any item may have several others linked to it. The memory chain technique works nicely for branched lists. For instance, if the key word *hammer* is simultaneously linked to *beer, bell,* and *pudding,* you can easily visualize multiple associations to recall this linkage.

The full procedure, therefore, is to memorize core points with a memory chain and then treat each core point as the first item in a branched list. As usual, use vivid substitute images and imaginative associations.

EXERCISES

1. The thought maps in Figure 10.1 describe the organization of a stage play. Use the procedure of this section to memorize and reproduce these maps. (It is not necessary to understand the maps to do this exercise. Naturally, it is easier to remember a meaningful map you developed yourself.)

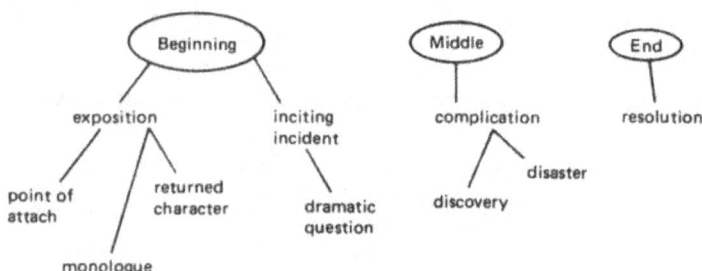

FIGURE 10.1

2. Memorize and reproduce the thought maps you developed for the reading exercises at the end of the last chapter.

SUMMARY

Notes as abstracts: Writing extensive, literate condensations of information can impede learning.

Taking notes: A thought-map format for notes assists learning and remembering. A compact but interesting map structure is best; use abbreviations and visual embellishments. Gradually improve note taking by relying more on key words and less on exposition.

Studying notes: Thought-map notes are treated by telescoping. (1) The thought-map cores are linked in a memory chain. (2) Subordinate items are linked to the cores in branched memory chains.

EXERCISE

Develop and memorize thought maps for the following chapter. See whether you can think through all the important points—or, if you can find a very patient ear, deliver a detailed monologue.

PART

IV

SPECIAL APPLICATIONS

Part IV presents applications of more specialized interest; however, each contributes to your effectiveness as a skillful learner even though you may not require that particular application. For this reason, I suggest you don't dismiss a chapter such as Chemical Structures without at least a partial reading.

11

■

THE

BRAIN

■

Applications of brainbooster techniques utilize brain functions

■

This chapter is devoted to some of the findings of a variety of disciplines that now are loosely termed "cognitive sciences." The amalgam includes theories and research in brain physiology, memory, artificial intelligence, problem solving, and educational psychology. *The New Brainbooster* is a practical handbook of applied cognitive sciences.

BRAIN STRUCTURE

The human brain is the most complex device on this planet. It is a switchboard wired with some ten billion *neurons*, long slender cells that carry electrical impulses. Hundreds of fibrous branches, the *dendrites*, may radiate from the ends of a neuron, connecting it with other neurons in a dizzying network.

The interior portions of the brain govern the most primitive activities: the monitoring, coordination, and control of bodily processes and some basic emotions. Higher functions are invested in the outer portion of the brain, the *cortex*. The folds and convolutions of the cortex give the brain its familiar appearance of a huge gray walnut. A map of the cortex shows areas associated with vision, hearing, touch and muscle control, smell and taste, and language. It contains 75 percent of the brain's neurons, all of which must be fed by a rich blood supply. Somehow, in ways not yet understood, the cortex thinks and learns.

About 25 percent of the calories we consume are spent to fuel the brain. The laws of thermodynamics demand that systems must spend energy to organize and build structures. All life therefore expends energy to maintain its structure, but the brain devours energy some ten times faster than other tissues. This is a vast expenditure to support a vast organization, a dynamic structure of chemical changes, dancing electrical impulses, and enough conducting fibers to girdle the world four times.

Your brain improves with use and, with some care and some luck, it can be more powerful than ever with advancing years. Most of the brain's flexibility lies in the possibility of improving its "programming"—in a word, learning. Concepts and information are probably chemically inscribed in new patterns and pathways for electrical messages. Each new pattern may be associated with old patterns, so that prior learning makes new learning easier.

Rats developed a thicker, heavier cortex when they were

given a rich environment of toys, ramps, wheels, and the like. Very likely a similar enrichment takes place in humans exposed to mental stimulation. Ordinarily, the aging brain may suffer a minor loss of neurons and a decline of certain chemical quantities. It now seems likely that such declines can be more than compensated for by a vigorous intellectual life and with good nutrition and life-style. People engaged in creative and educational pursuits often continue their intellectual growth throughout life.

TWO BRAINS

Your brain is both a logician and an artist. The logician is the left hemisphere, the analytic computerlike half of your brain that speaks, does arithmetic, and analyzes problems step by step. The artist is the right hemisphere, the imaginative, creative, and visual half of your brain. This hemisphere organizes thoughts in patterns and sees things whole.

Some bold contrasts can be seen by comparing the functions of the logical left brain and the artistic right brain:

Left Brain	Right Brain
Thinking with words: vocabulary, reading, and writing	*Thinking with images:* visualization, spacial relations, drawing.
Serial processing: step-by-step thinking, as in arithmetic.	*Simultaneous processing:* grasping things all at once, like recognizing faces.
Logical thinking.	*Intuitive thinking.*
Analysis: breaking things into components.	*Synthesis:* fusing components into an integrated whole.

This is a somewhat simplistic listing, but it will do for our discussion. Although each hemisphere dominates particular functions, the other hemisphere has similar abilities, but in weak form. People who have lost speech due to a massive injury to the left hemisphere have, with therapy and fortitude, learned to speak again using the "mute" right hemisphere.

The hemispheres work together by sending messages back and forth through a bridge of nerves called the *corpus callosum*. When this is cut, the hand controlled by the left brain can write but not draw, whereas the other hand can draw but not write. Incidentally, the left hemisphere controls the right hand and vice versa; this does not appear related to left- or right-handedness.

Most schooling is aimed at the analytic left brain. Indeed, traditional education discourages right-brain functions— drawing and day-dreaming are crimes in the classroom. The creative hemisphere is not treated as part of the intellect! This is less surprising when one realizes that we communicate with language, the currency of the left brain. The left brain then has a window to other minds, while the mute right brain labors in the lonely attic of imagination. Thus Shakespeare's plays and Einstein's theories were conceived by the right hemisphere and written by the left.

Unlike traditional schooling, learning techniques tap the immense resources of the right brain. The telescopic approach and the various mnemonic techniques depend upon organization, visualization, and association. Organization is a result of synthesis, of putting the parts together and seeing them as an integral whole. Visualization and visual associations are similarly right-hemisphere functions. Your deliberate efforts to use these principles in learning is akin to enlisting the help of an extra brain.

COMPONENTS OF MEMORY

Researchers recognize at least three components of memory: sensory, short-term, and long-term memories. Each has a distinctive role in capturing and storing information that we can use to further our efforts at remembering.

Sensory memory does not seem very much like a part of memory. It is a buffer that captures, for just a moment, all that you see, hear, and feel. Sensory memory holds an enormous amount of information, but only for a very short time (less than a second). You might glimpse a group of people and recognize a familiar face only after your eyes have left the scene. The scene had to be stored momentarily for your brain to perform this feat.

We capture information from sensory memory by focusing attention on it. This moves the sensory information into the conscious memory—the storage place of our current thoughts, our awareness. The conscious memory is brief, usually lasting only a few minutes under continual rehearsal. Because of this limited storage time, conscious memory is called *short-term memory* (although sensory memory is even shorter).

At any moment, short-term memory can hold about seven items, give or take two items. This means that you can telephone a seven-digit number immediately after hearing it, but not an unfamiliar ten-digit number. When you try to fill your short-term memory with excess items, some of the original items spill out. You may be interrupted after looking up a phone number, and the number flies from your mind.

The number of items in short-term memory is more important for remembering than is the information in these items. For example, the letters *C, P, S,* and the words *Cup, Pencil, Staple* are about equally easy to hold in conscious memory. Moreover, we are better able to remember the single word *CAPS* than the list *C,P,S.* This is one reason why acronyms are good mnemonic devices.

Other techniques also depend on the ability of conscious

memory to hold condensed information in chunks. Numbers, for example, are best remembered in groups of three or four digits; this is called *chunking*. Each stage in the telescopic approach, from the broadest outline to the smallest cluster of details, should contain few enough elements to be held entirely in short-term memory. Moreover, key words are summary devices that hold a lot of information in a single chunk.

Long-term memory is the storehouse of the brain—the component we most associate with learning. Its capacity is enormous, and some researchers now believe that long-term memory is virtually permanent. They believe that forgetting is not primarily due to fading memory traces. Rather, the traces may be "lost" because we cannot find where we stored them. Techniques based on association are powerful because they forge hooks to fish out stored information.

One major factor that affects the retention and retrieval of information in long-term memory is organization. Organization is so essential to learning that we *must* impose artificial structure on material that does not have a clear natural organization. Our telescopic techniques systematically impose organization whether it is natural or artificial.

A second major factor for long-term memory storage is rehearsal. Repeated rehearsal in short-term memory moves the information into long-term memory. Rehearsal also reduces the rapid forgetting caused by the "interference" of new information. Most of us discovered the use of rehearsal early in life and repeated things over and over till they burned their way into our memories. Rehearsal is almost synonymous with conventional study. It will always be a most important and reliable tool, but other techniques can help you to markedly reduce this tedious practice.

■

12

REMEMBERING
PEOPLE

■

Substitute images
for remembered names
and faces

■

An ability to remember people is a tremendous asset in business and social life. It is a skill you can master.

The famous mnemonist Harry Lorayne routinely memorizes the names of hundreds of people in an audience! He tells of his early career as a magician, when he had to demonstrate his public appeal to a potential television sponsor. Lorayne was told to perform throughout the sponsor's offices so the employees could render a verdict. It was a disastrous day for illusions as trick after trick flopped. Fortunately, Lorayne knew the power of remembering people—he learned the names of all the employees and spoke to each one. His new friends overlooked the flaws in his performance and gave him a rave review.

Dale Carnegie asserted that people have a fundamental need for recognition and appreciation. His book *How to Win Friends and Influence People* carried the message in seventeen editions within the first few months of its publication in 1937. Carnegie taught that a key to success is to give people the attention and approval they crave. This includes remembering and using the other person's name because "a man's name is to him the sweetest and most important sound in any language."

Some detractors think this approach is cynical and simplistic, but I have not heard it criticized for being wrong. Surely it is not so bad to foster an interest in others and to look for something praiseworthy in them. And, after all, the truth is not less valuable for being simple.

THE BASIC IDEA

Mrs. Bump has a bump on her nose, and Mr. Redwave has wavy red hair. You remember these people easily because they are described by their names. Although most names are not such descriptive labels, your imagination can make them so.

For example, Mr. Fox may have perfectly regular features, but you can imagine him with large canine ears and a long, foxlike snout. Ms. Smith can be imagined carrying a blacksmith's anvil. The name *Warnke* sounds like *worn key*, an easily visualized object. You can associate Mr. Warnke with his name simply by imagining a worn key projecting from his hair or nose or any prominent feature. These examples illustrate the technique for remembering names: create an image that reminds you of the name and associate the image with the person.

Use this procedure to remember the names of the people in Figures 12.1 through 12.4. In each case the name sounds like something visualizable. Associate the substitute image and the person in any bizarre way. The people involved won't mind your imaginative treatment (if you don't tell them about

FIGURE 12.1. Warnke

FIGURE 12.2. Lance

FIGURE 12.3. Chambers

FIGURE 12.4. Shu

it). After you have associated the names and faces, cover the captions, and check that you can recall the names in reverse order.

THE COMPLETE TECHNIQUE

How can you remember names that do not sound like objects? You can create substitute images that remind you of part or all of the name. For example, *Turner* can be replaced by *turnip*, and the name *Serifin* might be approximated by *seared fin* or *surfing*. With a small effort, your natural memory will reconstruct the original name from the substitute image.

The substitute images can be simple or very complex. The names *Mary* and *Paul* might be converted to *marry* (imagine Mary in a bridal gown) and *pail* (imagine Paul with a pail on his head). You want to concentrate on the sound rather than the spelling. To remember *Veniaminovich*, you might substitute *when I am in a ditch,* and *Sheresheveskii* can be built from *share a shaver's ski*.

Most often, the match between name and image is not very close. But almost any fragments that remind you of the original sound will work. *Car* works for *Carla* or *Carl*, and *point* should be sufficient for *Poindexter*. You can simply remember to fill out the actual name from these cues.

Try this technique to associate the names and faces in Figures 12.5 through 12.8. Remember that vivid imagery is the most important element in this technique. Review once, and then test yourself by covering the captions.

EMBELLISHMENTS

When it is difficult to think of a substitute image with the "right" sound, a rhyme can be equally useful. Some examples:

FIGURE 12.5. Serifin

FIGURE 12.6. Murphy

FIGURE 12.7. Mendez

FIGURE 12.8. Gibson

bones for *Jones*, *warts* for *Schwartz*, and *plant tin* for *Blanton*. The rhymes do not have to be very close to the name to work well.

It helps to link substitute images to a person's most outstanding feature. Robert has curly hair, so we can imagine a robber's mask protruding from his curls. Carla's big eyes may

99

be seen as the headlights of a car. When you meet these people again, the features that first caught your attention will remind you of their names.

Use substitute imagery to remember the names and faces in Figures 12.9 through 12.12. Review once, and then test yourself by identifying all the people in Figure 12.13 (pages 102–3.).

FIGURE 12.9. Blanton

FIGURE 12.10. Schwartz

FIGURE 12.11. Jones

FIGURE 12.12. Giordano

ADVICE ABOUT NAMES

Remembering names is a formidable task when you are introduced to dozens of people in a matter of minutes. A whirl of grins and handshakes usually accompanies introductions that are only half heard. If you are intent on remembering names, you must slow the introductions enough to hear the names pronounced clearly. People appreciate your interest when you ask them to repeat their names for clarification.

Even in the best circumstances, it takes time to develop adequate substitute images. At first they may take as much as a minute or two, too long for rapid introductions. Nevertheless, you can digest scores of names immediately by obtaining, in advance, a list of people that you expect to meet at a gathering. As introductions are made, simply associate the prepared images with the new faces.

FIGURE 12.13. This is a composite of all twelve photographs.

13

■

CHEMICAL
STRUCTURES

■

Telescopic techniques for
learning amino acid
structures in minutes

■

Some biologists say that DNA
molecules are life's most basic chemicals. After all, genetic
messages of unimaginable antiquity are written in DNA—the
blueprints of the living cell. Other students of nature see
energy transformations as the pivotal activity of life. They
naturally revere ATP, the energy-laden molecules that drive
biological reactions. Still others, like me, hold the romantic
notion that enzymes are life's central chemicals.

Of course, life does not reside in individual molecules. It is
their organization and their orchestration that somehow plays
life's song. Here enzymes are the players, the conductor, and

the music. Enzymes are produced from DNA instructions and are fueled by ATP, but it is the enzymes that conduct the main business of life:

Q. What chemicals extract energy and material from nutrients?

A. Enzymes.

Q. What chemicals are produced from this energy and material?

A. Enzymes.

Q. What chemicals control and regulate this production of enzymes?

A. Enzymes.

Much as English words are chains of various combinations of twenty-six letters, enzymes are chains of various combinations of twenty-odd chemical units called *amino acids*. College biology students routinely learn the names and structures of these amino acids. In this chapter you will apply techniques to learn seven of these and the approach can be extended to learning any complex chemical diagrams.

BACKGROUND

The atoms that occur most frequently in amino acids are symbolized by H (hydrogen), O (oxygen), N (nitrogen), and C (carbon). In drawings of the chemical structures, these symbols have line segments attached to represent bonds (each bond consists of a shared pair of electrons):

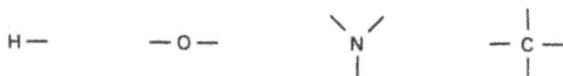

In chemical diagrams, the atomic symbols are joined together by their bond lines. Of course, each atom must have the correct number of bonds, as shown.

Amino acids have the structure summarized in the following diagram. Here the symbol R represents any one of twenty-odd different chemical "side chains." Notice that each atom has the correct number of bonds, but O-H is written in typical shorthand notation as OH. Some amino acid structures are listed in Figure 13.1 for reference. They are the structures you will learn in this chapter.

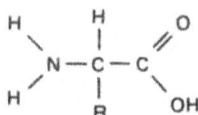

SIMPLIFYING THE DIAGRAM

You can use telescopic and substitute image techniques to reproduce the structures from the names and vice versa. The telescopic approach requires that you first reduce the structures to a bare outline. This is the procedure: (1) Since each amino acid contains the following grouping,

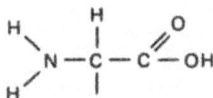

ignore the details of this structure and replace it with a rectangle. (2) Ignore all the confusing hydrogen atoms because they can always be added last to complete the structure. (3) Finally, reduce the next most repetitive symbol, C, to a dot. The result is shown in Figure 13.2.

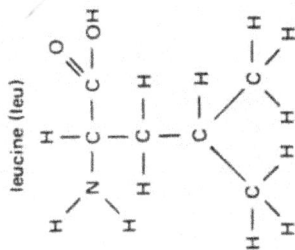

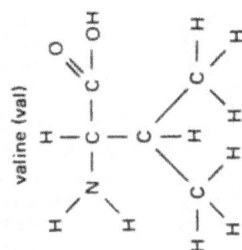

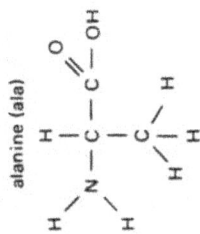

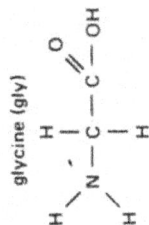

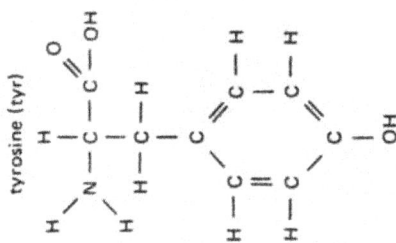

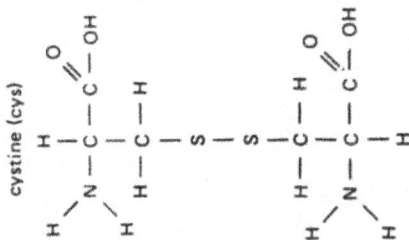

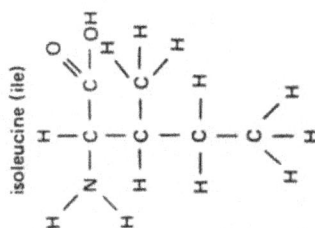

FIGURE 13.1

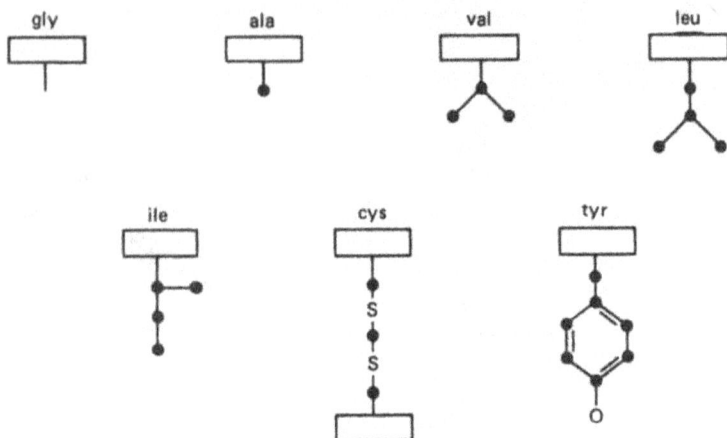

FIGURE 13.2

EXERCISE

Reconstruct the full structural diagrams for valine and leucine from their reduced diagrams (*not* from memory—that comes later). Check your results against the original diagrams.

Finally, reduce the diagrams to a still more bare outline by omitting the upper rectangles (Figure 13.3):

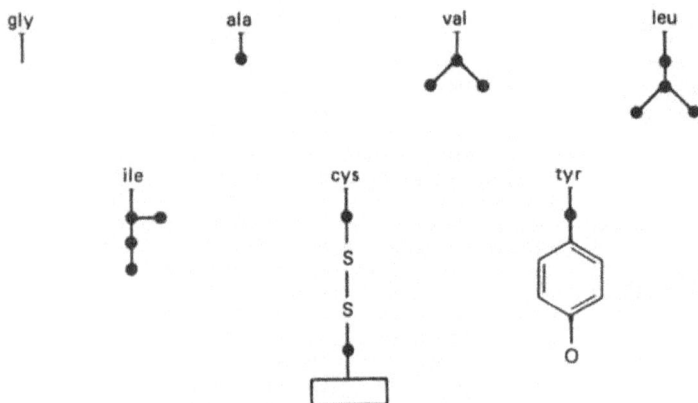

FIGURE 13.3

These structures are far simpler to memorize than the originals, and the successive layers of detail can be reconstructed easily.

EXERCISE

Reconstruct the original diagrams of glycine and isoleucine from the fully reduced diagrams (but not yet from memory).

MEMORIZING THE DIAGRAMS

You can now memorize the reduced diagrams using substitute images. For example, the word *glider* reminds me of *glycine*, so I imagine a glider with a long vertical line (representing the reduced diagram) hanging from it. The word *ale* reminds me of *alanine*, and I visualize a bottle of ale with a large dot on it. Similarly, a *veil* with three spots forming an inverted V is a substitute image for *valine*.

EXERCISES

1. Use the suggested images to recall the fully reduced diagrams for glycine, alanine, and valine.
2. Develop your own substitute images for leucine and isoleucine. Use your images to recall the fully reduced structures from the names alone. Take the time to create vivid images—even if you spend as much as three minutes on each structure, you can memorize twenty amino acids in an hour!

THE COMPLETED PROCESS

The last detail in reconstructing the originals from the reduced diagrams is to remember the characteristic "rectangle." A reduced diagram for this is

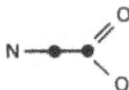

This is not pretty, but it is relatively easy to memorize. Of course, if you recognize the amine and carboxyl groups, you see this as,

Amine ——•—— Carboxyl

which is a greater reduction and is easier to remember.

EXERCISES

1. Draw from memory the full structural diagrams for glycine, alanine, valine, leucine, and isoleucine.
2. Use the full procedure to learn cystine and tyrosine. Draw their full structures from memory.
3. Recall the amino acid names from the complete structures.

14

■

WRITING

■

Mapping and other techniques make writing clearer and more effective

■

Writing sends thoughts from one mind to another across time and distance. Good writing transmits the thoughts clearly, accurately, and with a regard for the readers' efforts.

Conventional writing courses and texts abound with techniques and advice to attain these goals. A few of the most basic techniques and guidelines are given here—they can help in the mechanical process of writing and in the quality of the product.

ORGANIZING WRITING

Good organization makes writing easier and clearer. A detailed plan lets you concentrate on writing faster and more purposefully. Systematic techniques for organizing and outlining are naturally more useful for articles and reports than for shorter memos and letters. Still, good organization is important for all expository writing—regardless of brevity.

You uncovered the organization of readings with thought maps. The mapping process can be reversed so that you begin with maps and develop the writing from them.

Much of the work is done by ordering points on index cards. First write all the points you want to make on the cards. (Index cards are available at stationery stores.) Assign one point to a card. Recognize that the points on the cards are notes to yourself—do not spend much time or energy turning them into acceptable prose. That comes later.

Separate the cards into groups of closely related points. Cards for an article about vitamins, for example, are grouped so that points about vitamin C are separated from points about vitamin E, and so on. Now order the points within each group in the most logical sequence, so that one point ushers in the next. When the points are not logically connected, order them according to their importance. The most important point is usually put first. However, when you are building an argument or seeking a dramatic effect, reverse the order to culminate with the most important point.

Each group of cards now corresponds to a core point, and the individual cards correspond to the various subordinate points. Write the core point on a covering card for each group of cards. This step encourages you to see your writing in broad central points. Writing is more coherent with such core points in mind, and transitions are helped by referring to the core point. Suppose, for example, that a core label is "Stock Growth Indicators." The section might begin "Stock growth is indicated by several numbers . . . ," and later paragraphs might open with "Another number . . ." and "Growth is also reflected by. . . ." Throughout the section, the unity and flow of the writing is helped by occasional references to the core point.

Finally, organize the core points. These too can be ordered according to a logical sequence or order of importance. The ordered pile of cards is your outline. Translate the outline into thought maps to get a visual perspective of the whole unit. The time you spend organizing will be repaid generously during the writing process.

THE MECHANICS OF WRITING

Editing is easier than writing. Much easier. This is a key fact to consider in writing a rough draft.

Write a rough draft rapidly from your maps and cards. Try to get the whole story told with little concern for phrasing, transitions, or brevity. Do not struggle with fine points of clear writing—after all, you are going to rewrite. It can be difficult to write quickly; only a few writers fly through the rough draft, while others rise only to glacial rates.

New ideas often flash into mind as you write. Record them. Revisions in organization may also suggest themselves. If they are good, incorporate them. Some specialists believe you should formulate all your thoughts during the writing process; in their view, a rough draft should be written *before* the outline. My approach is more conventional, but flexible enough to allow you to incorporate new ideas and structural changes during writing.

Write the introduction *last*. An introduction can serve various purposes: (1) to orient the reader to the subject and its value, using historical, anecdotal, and factual background; (2) to stimulate interest in the subject; (3) to state the purpose of the writing; (4) to summarize results, conclusions, or recommendations; (5) to announce the plan of the material. The introduction to a chapter or section may use only one or two of these elements, while the introduction to a full report or article may include them all. In every case, writing the introduction is easier after the body has been developed.

When you complete the rough draft, put it away for a day or two so that you can read it more objectively. Then revise it.

The revision should have acceptable phrasing and transitions and should meet the guidelines for clear writing described in the following section. Simply put, it should be a readable manuscript. Many writers edit several more times, but it is rare for good writers to do without one revision. Even Isaac Asimov, one of the most prolific expository writers in the world, takes the time to do a rewrite.

WRITING FOR THE READER

Most readers want direct, informative articles that are free of jargon and pomp. Readers appreciate the use of simple past and present tenses, short paragraphs, and uncomplicated sentences. Expository writing can be entertaining, even occasionally poetic, and still hold to a spare, easy-reading style. These features are preferred because they save the readers' time and effort.

But there are important exceptions to this "easy-reading" style. Some nonfiction writing is meant to stimulate, persuade, or cause emotional responses. Some writings are part essay and part poetry. These forms presume the reader seeks more than naked ideas and information, and the author can enjoy more latitude to embroider with language.

An extreme is found in some technical writing that is filled with obscure terms and wordy, convoluted sentences. Often this is simply poor writing by specialists. Some disturbing studies suggest that muddy prose is being rewarded in college composition courses and that professionals tend to praise reports of work they do not understand. We need to recognize, however, that specialized legal, financial, medical, and academic articles need very accurate wording and that readers are willing to sacrifice time and effort for a bit more precision. Technical jargon has a proper place in such literature because it is easily understood by the specialist-readers.

Ideally, your writing level should match your readers' knowledge of the subject. If you are a specialist writing for specialists, you must write in the appropriate idiom. Writing for the general public is more difficult, because you cannot assume readers have your background—or interest—in the subject. You need to write at a level they can understand. Readers want information, not a show of the author's knowledge.

Moreover, while writers must reach out to readers, they should not reach down. Readers are intelligent beings and deserve not to be offended by condescension.

It comes to this: all writing attempts to communicate; good writing attempts to communicate with people.

STREAMLINING WRITING

Writing becomes clearer and easier to read when it is made simpler, less wordy, and more direct. Here I want to mention a few guidelines to help streamline writing.

Stick to your outline. Let the bones of your organization show through your writing. A clear outline, closely followed, is as much a map for your readers as for you.

Cut unnecessary words, phrases, and sentences. If the phrase or sentence does not amplify or improve your mes-

115

sage, strike it out. Writer Kurt Vonnegut refers to this as having the "guts to cut." It does take guts to cut words that once sounded so pretty and right. Cut them for your readers' sake.

Any sentence that uses many words to express a small thought is a likely candidate for trimming. Example: "Good organization makes writing easier for the writer and clearer for the reader." I edited this to "Good organization makes writing easier and clearer."

Weak qualifying phrases are another widespread source of fat. Sentences read better without them: "As the portability of computers grows, the concept of education ~~as it applies to many skills~~ will change."

Words can be streamlined too. Plain, familiar words are easiest to read. This means you might replace *adhere* with *stick* and *ubiquitous* with *widespread*. Of course, you won't always want to simplify vocabulary, but simplification usually helps the reader direct attention to the message rather than to the words.

15

■

NUMBERS

■

Remember telephone numbers, prices, dates, and long numbers of all kinds

■

Numbers are notoriously difficult to memorize. A few numbers are easily remembered because they contain predictable sequences such as *2468* or symmetrical patterns such as *141414*. Most often, however, numbers are bloodless ciphers without pattern or visual appeal.

Elaborate mnemonic devices have been developed to cope with the problem of numbers. One popular system was developed (as far as I can tell) by Dr. Bruno Furst and is widely used by modern mnemonists. This method assigns sounds to the digits; numbers then become words or word

117

lists that are easily recalled. It is a powerful approach, but requires substantial practice to master.

The method presented here is more direct and can be thoroughly learned in one sitting. This technique of *animated digits* is as powerful as any for rapid learning. No doubt it is an old technique, but I have not seen it described explicitly.

THE TECHNIQUE
OF ANIMATED DIGITS

Once again we can discover a powerful memory device by examining the approach of the incredible Russian mnemonist, Sheresheveskii. Unlike most of us, he found numbers to be the *easiest* items to remember, and he could memorize number lists without apparent limit.

Sheresheveskii regarded digits not as abstract symbols but as colorful characters. He saw the number 6 as a man with a huge swollen foot and 8 as a fat woman. Probably Shereshev-eskii imagined long numbers as scenes being played by these digit-actors; the number 868 may be seen as two fat women crushing a man (with a swollen foot) between them. We can extend this basic idea to remember any number.

Press your imagination to see the following digits as characters and objects:

0   an egg
1   a police officer standing at attention (wearing a cap)
2   a floating swan with curved neck
6   a man with a swollen foot
8   a fat woman

Follow the imagery given here to remember the number *26102881600*: A large swan has a man (with a swollen foot) riding on its back (26). This surprises a policeman sitting on an enormous egg, which breaks open and hatches a golden swan (*102*). The golden swan is promptly chased by two fat sisters and a policewoman (*881*). In the chase, they step on a man's swollen foot, angering him and causing him to throw two eggs at them (*600*). Use vivid imagery, and recall the original number from your memory of the scenes.

Questions can arise regarding the order of the digits; do a police officer and an egg represent *10* or *01*? A natural way to keep track is to place the character-digits in the same left-to-right positions as they occur in the number. If the number is *10*, then the officer is seen to the left of the egg. When you want the placements to be vertical—say a man riding a swan—have the character representing the first digit reach highest in the scene. Thus to represent *26* you imagine a man on a swan with the swan's head above the man's. (Of course, it is even easier to imagine *26* as a swan riding on a man's shoulders.)

Let the character-digits face any direction that suits you. A 2 looks like a swan facing left, but it can face right in any scene you imagine.

EXERCISE

Use the technique of this section to memorize the number *8012068216* *within three minutes.*

We can now complete the list of digits. Again, extend your imagination to these:

0   an egg
1   a police officer
2   a swan
3   a butterfly (the loops are wings)
4   a girl (her hand is on her hip so the bend in the 4 is her elbow)
5   a snake
6   a man (with a swollen foot)
7   a cane or walking stick

8   a fat woman
9   an elephant (the loop is its ear and the stem is its trunk)

Be sure to create vivid, unusual images. In your mind's eye a walking stick can walk, a butterfly can be as big as an eagle, and an elephant can lay eggs. Animated objects such as an egg with legs or a talking cane are always useful elements. When possible, invent a story for each scene; the better the story, the stronger your recall. You can vary your character-digits by changing their color, composition, dress, and size. It also helps to see the numbers in groups (scenes) of two, three, or four digits.

EXERCISES

1. Use the technique of this section to memorize the number *6483591207*.
2. Take a brief rest, and then give yourself three minutes to memorize the number *132315759408698072*.

NUMBER ASSOCIATIONS

Useful numbers such as stock prices or telephone numbers must be associated with the appropriate names. Numbers and names are easily linked by familiar techniques.

As an example, the telephone number of Mr. Frog is 890-3167. You can remember this by imagining that Mr. Frog kisses a fat woman (8) who is being pushed by an elephant (9), etc. This links Mr. Frog with his telephone number.

EXERCISES

1. Relate the following names and telephone numbers. Rehearse once for each and then cover the numbers and recall them from the names alone:

Mr. Frog	890-3167
Ms. Bear	420-5006
Dr. Owl	589-1366

2. Use the same approach as in Exercise 1 to remember the following historic dates:

Mohammed's flight from Mecca	622
Black plague reaches Europe	1347
Birth of Ludwig van Beethoven	1770

Cover the dates and recall them from the events.

By now you may have noticed that you remember many numbers even without a rehearsal. The technique promotes close attention and deep memory traces.

SUMMARY

Animated digits: To remember numbers, visualize scenes with the digits as colorful characters or animated objects:

0 egg	5 snake
1 police officer	6 man
2 swan	7 cane
3 butterfly	8 fat woman
4 girl	9 elephant

Number associations: Numbers can be associated with names by linking an image for the name to the number images.

PART

V

■

MENTAL
VIDEORECORDING

■

The next three chapters show how to absorb lectures, presentations, and motion pictures without notes. Most often, I recommend note taking over this technique because it is easier and more reliable. Of course, when you are comfortable and confident with mental videorecording, it is a spectacular tool. It is particularly useful for giving speeches without notes.

■

16

■

MEMORY

PEGS

■

A variation of substitute imagery for mental videorecording

■

Ancient Greek orators gave long detailed speeches without notes or cue cards. They associated ideas with the objects in a house. The orator imagined himself walking through the house and, as each object arose in his mind, he recalled the corresponding phrase. Objects such as doors, cabinets, and chairs served as mental pegs on which the orator could hang new images. This is an example of the memory peg technique, whereby you associate information with familiar objects.

MEMORY PEGS

Almost any object can serve as a memory peg—a kind of mental hook that stores information by association. Ideas are joined to the pegs as key words or substitute images. Try this exercise: For each item in the following list, make a vivid visual association with the object in the adjacent diagram. When you complete the associations, cover the word list but not the diagrams. Then see if you can recall the list from the diagrams alone.

Background	Key Words	Memory Peg
Dinosaurs and approximately 70 percent of all living species became extinct about 65 million years ago.	*Dinosaur dying* (suggestion: imagine a dying dinosaur smashing through the door)	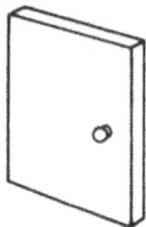
Many scientists believe the extinctions were caused by an asteroid that struck the earth.	*Asteroid* (suggestion: visualize a lamp-shaped asteroid plunging to earth)	
The asteroid crashed through the earth's crust and spewed huge clouds of dust and ash into the atmosphere.	*Dust and ash*	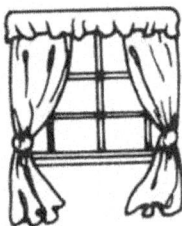
The dust cloud surrounded the earth, blocking the sun for a few years.	*Blocked sun*	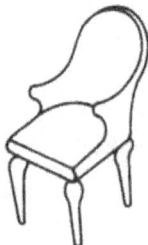

Widespread extinctions followed from (1) worldwide cooling, and (2) plants dying for lack of sunlight. Animals that fed upon these plants soon followed, as did the meat-eating animals that preyed upon the plant eaters.

Worldwide cooling

Plants died

Important evidence for the asteroid theory has been found in layers of rock. Generally, older rocks are deeper underground. Sixty-five-million-year-old rocks from around the world have been found to contain a thin layer of the element iridium, believed to be the fall-out of the dust cloud. Iridium is not generally found on the surface of the earth, so the iridium deposit is thought to be due to the asteroid.

Layers of rock

Iridium
(suggestion: a red yam)

DEVELOPING YOUR OWN PEGS

You can now recognize some of the advantages of memory pegs over memory chains. It takes less time to make associations with familiar pegs than with items in a chain. Moreover, items can be easily recalled out of sequence, and you can

127

safely forget various items without losing the whole list. Later I'll show that a combination of peg and chain techniques is most effective for applications such as public speaking and remembering lectures and presentations.

An obvious drawback to the peg technique is that you must memorize peg lists. One sophisticated version of the peg technique uses numbers as pegs. This is a powerful approach because it imposes numerical order on the items, and the pegs are never exhausted. Nevertheless, this version takes considerable practice, and the extra benefit is probably not worth the extra effort. The system discussed here can be learned and used immediately.

I recommend an approach like that of the ancient Greek orators (referred to as the method of *loci*). Choose a room that is very familiar to you; perhaps a bedroom, kitchen, or office. Briefly review features and objects in the room in a definite sequence—perhaps starting with a door and working your way along the walls recording windows, decorations, and furniture along the way. Then you may spiral into the interior of the room, noting rugs, tables, chairs, lamps, etc. You must be able to visualize these pegs clearly, quickly, and in sequence.

Try to develop thirty or more pegs from one room. Use items that have somewhat permanent locations in the room. Do not use identical items in close proximity, such as dining-room chairs or books on a shelf, because they can become indistinct in your memory. Rather, choose just one or two such identical objects and ignore the others.

Memory pegs can be used repeatedly to store different information. The pegs cannot be used twice in the same day, however, because the associations interfere with each other. Remarkably, the peg associations made a day apart seldom cause confusion.

If you find later that you need more than one set of pegs, you can develop them from other rooms. The pegs can also be objects that you encounter on a familiar walk or ride. Sheresheveskii placed list items along remembered routes— in a doorway, under a street lamp, against a fence. You will find, as he did, that it helps to exaggerate the pegs and associations. Even the illumination that you visualize is important because you can "overlook" an item like an egg in an unlit doorway.

NUMBERS AS PEGS

Some mnemonists use numbers as memory pegs. One obvious advantage is that items are remembered in numerical order. To see how this works, suppose you want to remember a numbered list: (1) *table*, (2) *letter*, etc. you can visualize as an officer (1) growing out of a table, a swan (2) eating a letter, and so on. Multiple-digit items require composite scenes. For example, item 84, *balloon*, can be seen as a fat woman and a young girl flying in a balloon. (See chapter 15 to review the technique for numbers.)

EXERCISE

To obtain a feeling for numerical pegs, associate the items below with the given numbers:

(1) table	(11) dog	(65) apple
(2) letter	(22) pencil	(78) microphone
(10) eyeglasses	(23) tree	(84) balloon

Now cover the list and recall the items associated with the following numbers: *11, 23, 84, 1, 2, 10, 22, 65, 78.*

The technique can be used to remember pages in a book or magazine. Page ten may have a picture and report on fashionable eyeglasses. You can associate *10* with this information, and when someone calls out "page ten," you can describe the contents of the page, including the layout and the photographs. It is a very theatrical stunt.

USING PEGS

Memory pegs are useful for giving speeches and for absorbing lectures, presentations, films, and the like. These applications are presented in more detail in the next two chapters.

Of course pegs can also store information from readings. Most reading to remember should be recorded on thought maps because maps are permanent records in unlimited supply, unlike pegs. Still, the peg system is a convenient writing-free way to record some uncomplicated readings. More important, using pegs for reading material is good practice for the other applications.

The most tidy and economical use of pegs is to attach core points to them. The subordinate points can then be linked to the cores by memory chains. The effect is to create a kind of thought map on each peg. These maps should be kept simple for applications requiring rapid memorization or recall. Elaborate maps take longer to invent and decode.

SUMMARY

Memory pegs: Almost any object can serve as a memory peg. When information is associated with these, they serve as cues. The peg stimulates recall of the information.

Developing pegs: Memory pegs are most easily formed from features and objects of a familiar room. It is desirable to develop about thirty pegs. Memory pegs can be used repeatedly for different information. However, they *cannot* be used to record information twice on the same day.

Using pegs: Associate core points with memory pegs, and link the subordinate points to these in memory chains.

EXERCISES

1. Check your recollection of about thirty pegs.
2. Without writing any notes, record the following article on memory pegs. Check to see that you remember the main points.

How to Write with Style by Kurt Vonnegut

Newspaper reporters and technical writers are trained to reveal almost nothing about themselves in their writings. This makes them freaks in the world of writers, since almost all of the other ink-stained wretches in that world reveal a lot about themselves to readers. We call these revelations, accidental and intentional, elements of style.

These revelations tell us as readers what sort of person it is with whom we are spending time. Does the writer sound ignorant or informed, stupid or bright, crooked or honest, humorless or playful—? And on and on.

Why should you examine your writing style with the idea of improving it? Do so as a mark of respect for your readers, whatever you're writing. If you scribble your thoughts any which way, your readers will surely feel that you care nothing about them. They will mark you down as an egomaniac or a chowder-head—or, worse, they will stop reading you.

The most damning revelation you can make about yourself is that you do not know what is interesting and what is not. Don't you yourself like or dislike writers mainly for what they choose to show you or make you think about? Did you ever admire an empty-headed writer for his or her mastery of the language? No.

So your own winning style must begin with ideas in your head.

1. **FIND A SUBJECT YOU CARE ABOUT**

Find a subject you care about and which you in your heart feel others should care about. It is this genuine caring, and not your games with language, which will be the most compelling and seductive element in your style.

I am not urging you to write a novel, by the way—although I would not be sorry if you wrote one, provided you genuinely cared about something. A petition to the mayor about a pothole in front of your house or a love letter to the girl next door will do.

2. DO NOT RAMBLE, THOUGH

I won't ramble on about that.

3. KEEP IT SIMPLE

As for your use of language: Remember that two great masters of language, William Shakespeare and James Joyce, wrote sentences which were almost childlike when their subjects were most profound. "To be or not to be?" asks Shakespeare's Hamlet. The longest word is three letters long. Joyce, when he was frisky, could put together a sentence as intricate and as glittering as a necklace for Cleopatra, but my favorite sentence in his short story "Eveline" is this one: "She was tired." At that point in the story, no other words could break the heart of a reader as those three words do.

Simplicity of language is not only reputable, but perhaps even sacred. The *Bible* opens with a sentence well within the writing skills of a lively fourteen-year-old: "In the beginning God created the heaven and the earth."

4. HAVE THE GUTS TO CUT

It may be that you, too, are capable of making necklaces for Cleopatra, so to speak. But your eloquence should be the servant of the ideas in your head. Your rule might be this: If a sentence, no matter how excellent, does not illuminate your subject in some new and useful way, scratch it out.

5. SOUND LIKE YOURSELF

The writing style which is most natural for you is bound to echo the speech you heard when a child. English was the novelist Joseph Conrad's third language, and much that seems piquant in his use of English was no doubt colored by his first language, which was Polish. And lucky indeed is the writer who has grown up in Ireland, for the English spoken there is so amusing and musical. I myself grew up in Indianapolis, where common speech sounds like a band saw cutting galvanized tin, and employs a vocabulary as unornamental as a monkey wrench.

In some of the more remote hollows of Appalachia, children still grow up hearing songs and locutions of Elizabethan times. Yes, and many Americans grow up hearing a language other than English, or an English dialect a majority of Americans cannot understand.

All these varieties of speech are beautiful, just as the varieties of butterflies are beautiful. No matter what your first language, you should treasure it all your life. If it happens not to be standard English, and if it shows itself when you write standard English, the result is usually delightful, like a very pretty girl with one eye that is green and one that is blue.

I myself find that I trust my own writing most, and others seem to trust it most, too, when I sound most like a person from Indianapolis, which is what I am. What alternatives do I have? The one most vehemently recommended by teachers has no doubt been pressed on you, as well: to write like cultivated Englishmen of a century or more ago.

6. SAY WHAT YOU MEAN TO SAY

I used to be exasperated by such teachers, but am no more. I understand now that all those antique essays and stories with which I was to compare my own work were not magnificent for their datedness or foreignness, but for saying precisely what their authors meant them to say. My teachers wished me to write accurately, always selecting the most effective words, and relating the words to one another unambiguously, rigidly, like parts of a machine. The teachers did not want to turn me into an Englishman after all. They hoped that I would become understandable—and therefore understood. And there went my dream of doing with words what Pablo Picasso did with paint or what any number of jazz idols did with music. If I broke all the rules of punctuation, had words mean whatever I wanted them to mean, and strung them together higgledy-piggledy, I would simply not be understood. So you, too, had better avoid Picasso-style or jazz-style writing, if you have something worth saying and wish to be understood.

Readers want our pages to look very much like pages they have seen before. Why? This is because they themselves have a tough job to do, and they need all the help they can get from us.

7. PITY THE READERS

They have to identify thousands of little marks on paper, and make sense of them immediately. They have to *read*, an art so difficult that most people don't really master it even after having studied it all through grade school and high school—twelve long years.

So this discussion must finally acknowledge that our stylistic options as writers are neither numerous nor glamorous, since our readers are bound to be such imperfect artists. Our audience requires us to be sympathetic and patient teachers, ever willing to simplify and clarify—whereas we would rather soar high above the crowd, singing like nightingales.

That is the bad news. The good news is that we Americans are governed under a unique Constitution, which allows us to write whatever we please without fear of punishment. So the most meaningful aspect of our styles, which is what we choose to write about, is utterly unlimited.

8. FOR REALLY DETAILED ADVICE

For a discussion of literary style in a narrower sense, in a more technical sense, I commend to your attention *The Elements of Style*, by William Strunk, Jr., and E. B. White (Macmillan, 1970). E. B. White is, of course, one of the most admirable literary stylists this country has so far produced.

You should realize, too, that no one would care how well or badly Mr. White expressed himself, if he did not have perfectly enchanting things to say.

17

■

SPEECH
MAKING

■

How to make and deliver
good speeches, lectures, and
presentations

■

Public speaking has many forms. Reports across the conference table, formal speeches, lectures, and presentations all have their special styles and durations. In each case one speaker addresses an audience of many. No other forum is as potent for instructing, influencing, and inspiring.

A few guidelines can help you to prepare and deliver effective talks. I focus on instructive lectures and presentations, but most of the discussion applies to any speech of twenty minutes or more. Brevity is an asset in almost any talk—try to keep your address under an hour. Even a highly interesting talk can turn sour when it runs too long.

Here I address four stages in the development and execution of a complete talk: organization, writing, practice, and delivery.

ORGANIZING THE TALK

The audience at your talk cannot reread passages for clarification. Once spoken, the information flies away at the speed of sound. This is a problem because people need to organize, correlate, compare, and reorder information in order to learn. Superior speakers assume the burden of keeping the organization and purpose before the audience, especially when the talk is technical.

A talk is divided into the *introduction,* the *main body,* and the *summation.* The introduction tells the audience what will be said; the main body says it; the summation tells what was said. Concentrate first on the organization of the main body.

Gather the material for your talk and write each of the points on a separate index card. Caution: it takes three or four times as long to deliver a talk as it does to read it; try not to include fine points that you will have to cut later due to time limitations. The cards are just notes to yourself, so do not bother to write them carefully for public address—yet.

Assemble the cards into small groups of closely related points—preferably less than six cards to a group. Order the cards within each group in either the most logical sequence or in ascending order of importance. Each group of cards now corresponds to a core point, and the cards within the group are subordinate points.

Label each card group with a covering core point card. Then order the core point groups either in the most logical sequence or in increasing order of importance. When the choice between these is not impelling, good rhetoric favors the ascending order of importance. The fully ordered pile of cards is your outline of the main body.

Make thought-map sketches from the outline. Each map should have a simple structure with few embellishments around the core. A talk needs to be simpler and easier to assimilate than written material because there is no opportunity to look back.

WRITING THE TALK

Write the main body of your talk from the maps and cards. Write as you would speak—not as you would write for an article. Keep your audience in mind throughout. How much do they know about the subject? How much detail can they digest in the limited time available? What is their interest in the subject? Do not aim for a level well above the audience's background—this sin can turn your talk into a lullaby. And if you simplify or popularize your topic, do so without condescension.

Experienced speakers may write very little and ad lib the rest. If you are new to the podium, you probably want to write every word of the speech. Write it on large index cards with each card reserved for one core point and its associated points. This format is very easy to study and physically limits the amount of "clutter" surrounding any core point. Don't write too much—remember that a talk takes much longer to deliver than to read.

Now write the summation on one or two index cards. Briefly summarize the highlights and theme of your talk. Make any projections or conclusions. Finish with a clear closing sentence or two. For example: "This concludes the discussion of cooperative quantum effects in chemical systems. Thank you very much," or "It's been a pleasure to speak to the Association today. Have a wonderful season."

The introduction is written last. It must orient the listeners to the subject and give the purpose and plan of the talk. Do so rather briefly and colorfully, if possible. An audience can lose interest quickly when the introduction is weak. Limit your writing of the introduction to three large index cards or less. Give a background discussion suitable for the level of the audience, reveal the purpose of the talk, and tell how you plan to do it. Mention the theme of the talk in words similar to those in the summation.

PRACTICING

A good speech *sounds* extemporaneous. Reading from notes erects a barrier between the speaker and audience with deadening effect. Many accomplished speakers *do* read prepared text, but their preparations are so thorough that the talk seems conversational and spontaneous—like that of an actor with memorized lines.

An address that is aired on radio or television must be scripted, because hesitations and awkward phrasings are magnified by these media. In other situations minor flaws actually make the talk more conversational and intimate. Regardless of the forum, talks are far more effective when they are memorized point by point. Veteran speakers avoid memorizing speeches word by word, because a practiced reading can give the same effect with much less effort. Exception: memorize the opening sentences in detail.

I recommend that you give speeches without notes. You can do this easily with the peg system; use one mental peg for every large index card. Prepare the pegs well enough to "read" them as you would cue cards. Even if you want written notes as a crutch, it helps your confidence and performance to have the points committed to memory.

Rehearse the speech until it is smooth. Time it without rushing, and trim when it is too long. On the other hand, a speech that successfully conveys your message cannot be too short.

ONSTAGE

If you are new to the speakers' podium, you should expect to suffer some anxiety—stage fright. You have this in common with the very best speakers. Stage fright usually diminishes with experience, but it rarely disappears. Don't worry about it; it won't kill you, and the tension will probably sharpen your performance. Concentrate on doing the job rather than on your emotions. After you deliver the first few memorized lines, you will settle into a much more controlled state.

Face the audience as you would a gathering of good friends. Generally, the larger the audience, the more appreciative it is. Approval and applause are contagious, and the approval is amplified in a large group. Appear as relaxed as possible, and don't rush. A smile can start you in the right direction (but not while giving a eulogy). Your main concern, once you've begun, is to *talk to the audience*. Do not hide behind words— think about getting your message across. It helps to focus your attention on a few responsive people throughout the audience.

Brief anecdotes and humorous remarks are usually welcome in speeches. But beware of telling jokes—comedians are highly vulnerable speakers.

18

■

LISTENING
AND VIEWING

■

**Mental recording of lectures,
TV shows, and motion
pictures—without notes**

■

Sometimes when I lecture on physics I find myself pacing on the podium and waving my hands in a storm of ideas and equations. Suddenly, my fervor fizzles as I glimpse the audience writing hurriedly, without looking up. They never really listened to my zealous performance.

The problem is a familiar one. A speaker can lope along at a rate faster than 100 words per minute—several times faster than most people can write. Serious listeners feel that they cannot remember the outpouring of ideas, so they attempt to transcribe the information and learn it later. This is usually a difficult and a wasteful procedure because writing diverts attention from thinking. Even when the writing succeeds, the product is likely to appear unfamiliar.

Instead of transcribing presentations word by word, you can either take notes or memorize the central features in a kind of mental videorecording. Certainly note taking requires less preparation and is more reliable because it produces a permanent record. Nevertheless, mental recording is an immediate and complete way to learn and remember. A permanent record can be made later upon rehearsing the material. Very likely you will find that you favor notes for some subjects and mental recordings for others. You can determine your preferences after some experimentation.

MENTAL RECORDING

Mental recording is an instrument for some impressive learning feats. Businesspeople use it to remember detailed presentations, students to absorb long lectures, viewers to relive their favorite motion pictures scene by scene—all after just one exposure and without formal study.

The basic idea in mental recording is to place important points on mental pegs. When the importance of a particular point is in doubt, it is stored on a peg to be on the safe side. The mental pegs you developed in chapter 16 put you only minutes away from being able to remember a news broadcast or documentary film in detail.

Each important fact or idea is likely to have subordinate points. These embellishments are most comfortably attached by a memory chain to the same peg as the core point, rather than using new pegs. This is like storing a simple thought map on each peg.

This mixing of memory pegs and memory chains conserves the pegs and imposes organization on the material as you receive it. In practice, some information may not be packaged as you expect; then you can relinquish the ideal format and catch the items on pegs alone.

EXERCISE

Make a mental record of a thirty-minute news broadcast or information program. Do not be overly concerned about memorizing unfamiliar names or terms—these need special attention. Patiently reconstruct as much of the program as you can. Some pegs can be blank at first, but, as you review other information, you may be reminded of the "missing" information.

NAMES AND TERMINOLOGY IN LISTENING

Mental recording is easy to do, with some exceptions. Unfamiliar names and terms are very difficult to digest from an outpouring of spoken words. The simplest solution is to write the names and terms. You can relate these to the appropriate pegs with only a modicum of concentration. Since most of my audiences are interested in techniques they can apply immediately, I recommend that they begin mental recording with a pen and paper backup.

Purists who insist on writing nothing must become proficient in using the substitute image technique rapidly. That is, they must first create a substitute image for a term and associate this with the appropriate peg. The procedure is familiar from memorizing readings, but the pace is dictated by the speaker. Keeping up takes plenty of practice.

ON LECTURES

The best feature of mental recording is that you can engage your mind rather than your pen. This does not apply to material that the speaker writes during a presentation, because you then have ample time for writing. I suggest that you transcribe most of what a lecturer writes, especially equations and diagrams. Of course, many experienced rapid learners take special pride in not writing anything—they put equations and diagrams on pegs. This is a showy demonstration, but it requires extra effort and is not necessary.

Lectures may be rich with information, so you should form associations only for information that is truly useful; this is essential for listening and viewing. Do not make special efforts to remember asides, embellishments, unessential details, or information that is familiar or obvious to you. New practitioners usually find they have abundant peripheral recall when they focus on central points.

As soon as possible, you should review the lecture and write it out in outline (thought maps are excellent for this purpose). You will find that this process is equivalent to hours of concentrated study by traditional methods.

A word of caution: do not rely on mental recording for important lectures until you have first practiced on several news or information programs. Even then, begin cautiously, with just one lecture per day. You can develop more pegs and handle more lectures as your ability and confidence grow.

VIEWING MEDIA

Note taking cannot rival mental recording for remembering highly visual media presentations such as motion pictures, stage shows, and television programs. For these the visual changes of scene are stronger cues than key words or even story lines.

A motion picture, for example, is most easily remembered by associating an exaggerated element from each scene with a memory peg. If a scene depicts people parachuting from a plane, then a vision of a tiny parachute would be a sufficient prod to remind you of the original scene. Remarkably, you may reconstruct an entire film so well that you notice connections or themes of which you were unaware in the actual viewing.

When information is somewhat dense, as it may be in an educational program, you must recall more than visual scenes. Usually it is quite sufficient to link memory chains of key images to the basic scenes. If there is too much detail in a scene to do this easily with a short chain, you are viewing a disguised lecture. Then simply forget about scenes as cues and concentrate completely on idea storage, as with any lecture.

SUMMARY

Mental recording: To assimilate presentations, convert central ideas and facts to images, and associate these with mental pegs. Attach subordinate points to the main point in a memory chain. Reconstruct the presentation patiently; seemingly blank spots will tend to fill in. Disregard unessential details and familiar or obvious information.

Names and terminology: It is easiest to write down unfamiliar names and terms. Otherwise, replace terms with substitute images and link them to pegs.

On lectures: Transcribe most material written by the lecturer, especially equations and diagrams.

Viewing media: Visual media are best absorbed by associating an exaggerated image from each scene with a peg.

EXERCISE

Practice mental recording of news broadcasts, motion pictures, and television presentations. (Do not use the same set of pegs more than once in a day.) When you are comfortable with the procedure, apply it to information-dense presentations and lectures.

PART

VI

■

PERFORM
INTELLIGENTLY

■

Here is a mixed bag of methods
to help your decision making,
problem solving, and teaching.

■

19

■

DECISION
MAKING

■

A procedure for making
better decisions

■

Decision-making techniques are typically tools for business management. Of course, making good decisions is not limited to business; personal decisions may route your journey through life.

The art and science of decision making is a significant subject. Executives who need sophisticated techniques either must know them or hire management consultants. Here I describe a simple and basic system of decision making that can be useful for the rest of us.

STATE YOUR GOAL

The basic process can be shown with a simplified example. Mr. Wise owns a small pharmacy in a resort area. He and another pharmacist manage well during the off-season, but they can barely cope with the increased business during the summer. An agency offers the services of pharmacists on a temporary basis at a premium price and Mr. Wise must decide how many, if any, temporary employees to hire.

It helps to have a general statement of your goal. In the pharmacy example it could be "hire the best number of temporary employees." Notice that this is not specific because it does not say what the "best number" means. Is it best for profit or best for Mr. Wise's health? This specification is the business of the next step in decision making, establishing criteria.

LIST THE CONSEQUENCES

"Establishing criteria" starts with listing all the possible consequences of your decision. Mr. Wise thought of three results of hiring additional pharmacists. He would have more time to rest and eat, his salary costs would be higher, and his customers would be better served during peak business hours.

It is standard practice for managers to list the consequences as *desirable* outcomes. The list then becomes a kind of wish list of outcomes from your decision—the criteria against which you test your goal. Experts refer to the list of positive consequences as *criteria* for this reason. Of course, Mr. Wise does not see "higher salary costs" as a desirable outcome, but it can be reworded to be a lesser evil as "lesser salary costs."

Now the criteria are put in order of importance and given a relative value on a scale of 0 to 10. Another scale of values like 0 to 4 would do as well. Usually these values are subjective; they represent how important each criterion is in relation to the others. Of course, some criteria can be equally important and have the same value.

148

Mr. Wise rates "more free time" as the most important outcome because his health suffers from the pressures of prolonged work hours and inability to eat regular meals. He assigns the maximum value of 10 to this criterion. Next in importance is "lesser cost" for which he chooses a value of 9. "Customer service" is weighed against the others and given a value of 4. Here is the list:

	Value (V)
More free time	10
Lesser cost	9
Customer service	4

LIST YOUR OPTIONS

A decision is a choice between options. In the pharmacy example these options are simply how many people to hire, if any. The options and the criteria are put together in a table as shown.

	Value (V)	Hire 0	Hire 1	Hire 2
More free time	10			
Lesser cost	9			
Customer service	4			

Expert decision makers stress that options are not always obvious. Some excellent decisions involve options that are inventive or unexpected. For example, a retired couple considered moving to where they could drive less than four hours to visit any of their scattered children and grandchildren. After some thought, they opted *not* to move but to learn to pilot a private plane. Now they can fly to their destinations in under two hours. The point is that choosing options can be a creative part of the process of decision making.

Options are rated on how well they meet the criteria using a scale of 0 to 10. In our pharmacy example, the "hire 0" alternative provides no free time, so this choice is given a 0. Mr. Wise feels that the "hire 1" choice would give him about 80 percent of the ideal amount of free time and assigns 8 to this option. There is a minimum time Mr. Wise must spend at the pharmacy, so a second hiring does not double his free hours. The "hire 2" option is assigned a value of 10.

Hiring two additional pharmacists would raise personnel costs by about 60 percent, so not hiring can be seen as "lowering costs" by that much. With this in mind, the "hire 0," "hire 1," and "hire 2" options are rated 6, 3, and 0, respectively. Mr. Wise also makes various subjective judgments rating the quality of customer service under each option. The entries are shown in the following table.

	Value (V)	Hire 0 (R)	Hire 1 (R)	Hire 2 (R)
More free time	10	0	8	10
Lesser cost	9	6	3	0
Customer service	4	4	7	8

THE DECISION

Some arithmetic shows the best choice. Multiply the criteria values (V) by the option ratings (R) as shown in the completed table below. The highest column total decides the best choice. In this case the "hire 1" option wins with a total of 135.

	Value	Hire 0		Hire 1		Hire 2	
	(V)	(R)	(V × R)	(R)	(V × R)	(R)	(V × R)
More free time	10	0	10 × 0 = 0	8	10 × 8 = 80	10	10 × 10 = 100
Lesser cost	9	6	9 × 6 = 54	3	9 × 3 = 27	0	9 × 0 = 0
Customer service	4	4	4 × 4 = 16	7	4 × 7 = 28	8	4 × 8 = 32
Totals			70		135		132

It is important that you do not blindly accept the results of your analysis. Be mindful that many of your numbers are subjective ratings and not immutable, accurate data. You must ask if the result of the process is reasonable. Does it agree with your expectations, and if not, why is it different? Feel free to go back and adjust values until you are satisfied that the decision is as good as you can make it. The process is meant to help you decide, not to dictate the decision.

20

■

S.O.S. FOR
PROBLEM
SOLVING

■

Techniques for solving verbal
problems in mathematics,
science, and business

■

Professional problem solvers spend years building a mental arsenal of techniques that they summon unconsciously when the need arises. Certainly no single chapter can treat very many of these "trade secrets." There are, however, three basic procedures that can immediately transform your ability to solve typical verbal problems in mathematics, science, and business: Symbolize, Organize, Simplify—the S.O.S. approach.

Most experts don't know how they solve problems. Research indicates that they use a telescopic approach, where they first ignore details and impose a central principle. In applying the principle, they treat subordinate questions, each of which may cascade into smaller questions. (Diagrams of this expert problem solving then look like thought maps with a central principle as the core and the subordinate steps as the branches.) The S.O.S. techniques help you solve problems in the professional manner.

In this chapter, the reader is assumed to know elementary algebra. Work your way through; it takes plenty of practice to become adept at problem solving.

SYMBOLIZE

A most elementary form of problem solving is to substitute numbers into an equation. If a principal of P dollars is invested at the yearly rate r, the yearly simple interest I is given by the equation

$$I = rP$$

This expression allows us to find any one of the three quantities, I, r, or P, from the other two. If, for instance, we know that interest is $240 and the rate is 12 percent, substitution in the equation gives

$$240 = .12P$$

and we find that the principal is $2,000. Problems like this are so trivial that novice problem solvers can overlook the importance of writing information in symbol form for less obvious cases.

Many problems, for example, are solved with the help of some standard equations, but which equations are used in a given case? This may be answered most directly by writing a list of all symbols for the quantities in the problem. The symbol list will indicate which equations to apply.

We can illustrate this with a set of equations that describes the motion of an object with constant acceleration a (the acceleration of a body is the change in its velocity divided by the duration of the change—a kind of rate of a rate). Physics texts usually present three equations for this purpose:

$$x = v_o t + \tfrac{1}{2} a t^2 \qquad (1)$$
$$v = v_o + at \qquad (2)$$
$$v^2 = v_o^2 + 2ax \qquad (3)$$

Here x is the distance (more precisely, the "displacement") through which the object moves, t is the time (duration) of the motion, v_o is the initial velocity of the object, and v is the later velocity of the object (after moving a distance x in time t). The choice of the "proper" equation depends on the problem.

Example: An astronaut stands on the moon and throws a rock vertically upward. It rises 1.2 meters in 1 second. If the downward acceleration of all objects near the moon's surface is 1.6 meters/sec², what was the velocity of the rock at the point of release?

Solution: Use a convention where upward displacements, velocities, and accelerations are positive, and all are negative when downward. Now simply translate the verbal information into symbol form:

Statement	Symbol
rises 1.2 meters	$x = 1.2$ meters
in 1 second	$t = 1$ sec
downward acceleration	$a = -1.6 \text{m/sec}^2$
velocity at release	$v_o = ?$

154

If possible, you want an equation that contains the unknown v_o, but no other unknown quantities. A glance at the symbol list for this example shows that equation (1) is the right choice. Substituting, we have

$$1.2 = v_o(1) + \tfrac{1}{2}(-1.6)(1)^2,$$

with the result that v_o is 2 meters/sec.

EXERCISE

A ball is thrown vertically upward at a velocity of 20 meters/sec and slows to 0.4 meters/sec after 2 seconds. Find the acceleration of the ball. *Answer:* -9.8 meters/sec^2. (Do not be concerned with units for the present.)

These straightforward problems show that symbolizing helps to identify the appropriate equation. In more difficult problems, the symbols also help to identify conditions needed to complete the problem. A list of the symbols can focus our attention on the "missing" symbols. These missing symbols correspond to conditions that are implied or assumed in the problem.

Example: A ball is thrown vertically upward at a velocity of 10 meters/sec. What is the maximum height it attains above the point of release?

Solution: As before, we list the obvious symbolic information:

Statement	Symbol
thrown at a velocity	$v_o = 10$ m/sec
maximum height	$x = ?$

Certainly, this begs for information if we are to use one of the three constant acceleration equations. These equations all contain acceleration a, so we must know or be given a value for a. Indeed, it is an important and surprising fact that all projectiles near the surface of the earth have a downward acceleration of 9.8 m/sec^2—whether they are rising or falling (assuming that air resistance is negligible). Our list now includes the value of a, but even this is not enough to solve the problem.

Equation (2) is not immediately useful because it does not contain the unknown, x. Equation (1) needs a value for t and equation (3) needs a value for v in order to give a complete algebraic solution. Is either t or v related to the "maximum height" condition of the problem? Consider that the highest point reached by the ball is the point where it stops momentarily, so $v = 0$ (this is not obvious, but it is true). The full list of symbols is now:

Statement	Symbol
thrown at velocity	$v_o = 10$ m/sec
maximum height	$x = ?$
fact: projectile acceleration	$a = -9.8$ m/sec
highest point condition	$v = 0$

This symbol list leads us to substitute into equation (3), with the result that x is approximately 5.1 meters.

EXERCISE

A ball is thrown vertically upward at a velocity of 19.6 meters/sec. How long does it take to reach its highest point?
Answer: 2 seconds.

Of course, not all problem conditions are numerical conditions like $v = 0$. Sometimes conditions are symbolic expressions like $L = 4W$. These can be included in symbol lists just like numerical data.

Example: The length of a rectangle is 4 times its width. The area is 100 cm. Find the width of the rectangle.

Solution: A general equation expresses the area A of a rectangle in terms of its length L and width W,

$$A = LW.$$

In order to solve for W, we need quantities or expressions for A and L. The list of symbols is:

Statement	*Symbol*
length is 4 times width	$L = 4W$
area is 100 cm	$A = 100$ cm
find the width	$W = ?$

Substituting into $A = LW$ gives

$$100 = 4W^2$$

with the solution $W = 5$ cm (and $L = 20$ cm). Notice that the only "new" step is to include a symbolic expression for L rather than a numerical value. Of course this simple problem can be done more directly, but the symbol-list approach works in difficult cases.

EXERCISE

The product of two positive numbers is 405, and one number is 5 times the other. Find the numbers. (Use the symbol-list approach of the last example.)
Answer: 9 and 45.

In many problems you must bear in mind that N unknowns require N independent algebraic equations for their solution. Thus, the last example could have been treated by seeing it as a problem with two unknowns, W and L. Then we would write the two necessary equations as

$$A = LW$$
$$L = 4W,$$

with the symbol list $A = 100$, $W = ?$, $L = ?$. When you have a choice, it is usually easier to treat problems as having one basic equation, with any other symbolic expressions put in the symbol roster.

ORGANIZE

You should attempt to organize all but the most elementary problems. Write the relevant equations in full before substituting any numbers. Draw any diagrams that may help. Make a symbol list as in the last section. See the problem as a special case of a general principle, and try to treat it as such.

Probably this advice is so obvious it seems trivial. But I believe that the greatest boost in problem-solving performance can come from a systematic approach to organization. When you first studied algebra, you learned to draw tables— tables for interest problems, tables for mixture problems, tables for age problems, ("If A is 12 years older than B was when C was twice as old as A will be . . ."), etc. These tables organize particular types of problems very nicely, but most of us have forgotten them. Worse, the tables are too specific— they do not show you how to organize new and unfamiliar problems. A more general approach to organizing problems is desired.

Most verbal problems have a core equation, a central condition expressed in algebraic terms. This core equation can be used as the spine around which the problem solution is organized. In the sciences core equations are laws expressed in equation form. They are particularly easy to recognize from the problem statements; a constant acceleration problem, for example, is sure to have its core equation among the three equations of the last section.

Some examples can show how various standard problems are organized around the core equation. The question that arises is, Which of several possible equations is a core equation? Almost any correct relation can serve as a core equation and can assist in problem organization, but the most useful expressions are usually the simplest, most obvious expressions.

Example: An investor with a $100,000 portfolio invests $40,000 at 6 percent and $35,000 at 8 percent. At what rate should the remainder be invested in order to yield a yearly interest of $7,000?

Solution: Although this is a simple problem, it illustrates the idea of a core equation. The most obvious relation is that the interest from three investments totals $7,000:

$$\text{Interest } A + \text{Interest } B + \text{Interest } C = 7,000.$$

This quite unspectacular expression can be used as a guide to write a symbol list:

$$\text{Interest } A = (\text{rate})\,(\text{principal}) = (.06)\,(40,000)$$
$$\text{Interest } B = (.08)\,(35,000)$$
$$\text{Interest } C = (\text{rate})\,(\text{remainder}) = r\,(25,000)$$

Now substitute these symbols into the core equation. A bit of algebra reveals $r = .072$, or 7.2%.

EXERCISE

A woman has $10,000 more invested at 7 percent than she has invested at 6 percent. Her annual income from these two investments is $2,000. How much is invested at 6 percent? (Use the core-equation approach.) *Answer:* $10,000.

Example: A does a job in 45 minutes. A and B together do the same job in 20 minutes. How long would it take B alone to do the job?

Solution: The core condition here is that the work rates add together so that

$$\text{Work rate } A + \text{Work rate } B = \text{Work rate together.}$$

To see this clearly, think of a transparent case where a worker does one job per hour and another does two jobs per hour; working together, they do three jobs per hour. Similar additive equations apply to the rates of filling storage tanks or the rates of filling and emptying highways.

As usual, a symbol list is organized around the core equation:

$$\text{Work rate } A = 1 \text{ job/45 min}$$
$$\text{Work rate } B = 1 \text{ job/t min}$$
$$\text{Work rate together} = 1 \text{ job/20 min}$$

Substituting these in the core equation and solving for unknown t gives $t = 36$ minutes.

EXERCISES

1. Three different pipes are used to fill a tank. Pipe A can fill it in 2 hours, pipe B in 3 hours, and pipe C in 6 hours. How long does it take for the three pipes together to fill the tank?
Answer: 1 hour.

2. The storage tank of the last exercise develops a leak that can empty it in 4 hours. How long does it take to fill the tank with the three pipes and the leak? (Notice that the new rate subtracts from the rate of filling.)
Answer: 1 hour, 20 minutes.

Example: How much 25 percent solution of acid should be mixed with 250 cc of 65 percent solution in order to obtain a 50 percent solution?

Solution: An equation that any mixture problem must satisfy is that the total material (acid in this case) is equal to the sum of material in all the parts. We can write

$$\text{Acid vol } A = \text{Acid vol } B = \text{Acid vol } C.$$

This condition is indirect because the problem statement does not mention the volumes of acid, only the volumes of the acid solutions. Use the symbol V for the unknown volume of the 25 percent solution. Then the volume of acid in the solution is given by $.25V$. The symbol list is developed from the core condition and the problem information:

$$\text{Acid vol } A = .25V$$
$$\text{Acid vol } B = .65\,(250)$$
$$\text{Acid vol } C = .5\,(250 + V)$$

Substituting from the list into the core equation gives the result $V = 150\text{cc}$.

EXERCISES

1. 320 kilograms of 45 percent copper alloy are to be mixed with an 85 percent copper alloy to obtain a 60 percent alloy. How many kilograms of 85 percent alloy are required?
   Answer: 192.
2. A confectioner has 6 kilograms of candy worth $4.00 per kilogram and 3 kilograms of another candy worth $5.00 per kilogram. How many kilograms of a third candy at $2.00 per kilogram must be mixed with these in order to have a mixture worth $3.50 per kilogram? (Notice that the core equation here is that the total cost of the mixture equals the sum of the costs of the components.)
   Answer: 5.

3. In a box of white balls and red balls, 8 more than half the total number of balls are red and 6 more than half the number of red balls are white balls. How many red balls does the box contain? *Answer:* 44.

When you use one core equation, write the symbol list in terms of only one unknown (one equation, one unknown). Similarly, for two core equations the list is written in terms of two unknowns, and so on. Part of the organization process is to adjust symbol lists into the proper form.

Example: A rectangle has a width 1 less than the length, and its area is 2 more than the width squared. Find the width.

Solution: When the area, A, of a rectangle is involved, we expect that a good core equation is the area equation:

$$A = LW$$

A first attempt at a symbol list gives the following:

Statement	Symbol
width 1 less than length	$W = L - 1$
area 2 more than width squared	$A = W^2 + 2$

If we were to substitute this directly into the core equation, both L and W would appear in the result. To correct this, simply rewrite the symbol list so that only L or W appears to the right of the equal sign (but not both). Manipulating $W = L - 1$ in the symbol list gives a new list:

$$L = W + 1 \text{ (from } W = L - 1)$$
$$A = W^2 + 2$$

Now substitution in the core equation results in $W = 2$.

EXERCISE

The altitude of a triangle is 3 more than one-half the base, and its area is 30 less than the square of the altitude. Find the altitude and the area of the triangle. (Recall that the area of a triangle is one-half base times altitude.)
Answers: 10, 70.

Another important step in problem organization is to draw diagrams and charts richly dressed with given information. The visual display often suggests core equations, and the labels help in formulating algebraic expressions.

Example: Car A leaves Los Angeles at 6:00 A.M. and travels at 60 miles per hour toward San Francisco, 400 miles away. Car B leaves San Francisco for Los Angeles and travels at 40 miles per hour. At what time do the cars pass each other?

Solution: A diagram (Figure 20.1) shows the distance between cities and the meeting point. The given information is all included in the diagram.

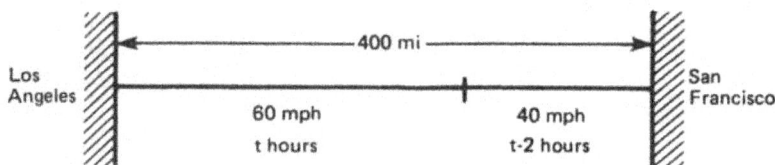

FIGURE 20.1

In particular, the time elapsed after 6 A.M. is labeled t. The core equation is obvious from the diagram:

Distance by A + Distance by B = 400 miles.

and the symbol list is equally evident from the labels:

Distance by A = 60 t

Distance by B = 40 $(t - 2)$

163

Substitution into the core equation gives $t = 4.8$ hours or 4 hours and 48 minutes. The cars meet at 10:48 A.M.

EXERCISE

A motorist drove 100 kilometers per hour on a country road and 60 kilometers per hour through town. A trip of 180 kilometers took 2 hours; how long was he traveling through town?
Answer: ½ hour.

Yet another approach to organizing a solution is to work backward. Imagine that you have the result, then ask yourself what step must immediately proceed it. If you can continue this process back to the beginning of the problem, the full solution is revealed. Working backward is especially useful for problems and puzzles that ask you to find a process to reach a desired goal.

Example: How can precisely 6 liters of water be measured with two containers, one with 9-liter capacity and the other with 4-liter capacity?

Solution: Let us draw the final situation first. This must be as follows:

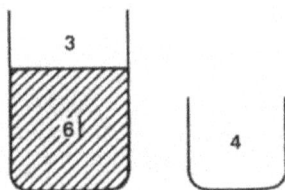

Immediately preceding this, the large container must have been full—after all, the only possible steps involve filling or emptying a vessel. In order for us to pour off only 3 liters, there must have been 1 liter in the small vessel:

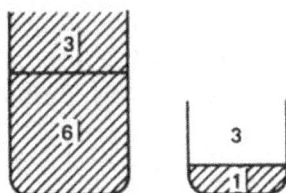

So now everything pivots on getting 1 liter of water in one of the containers. This is easily done by filling the smaller container from the large container twice:

Now simply reverse the steps and the problem is solved.

EXERCISE

How can precisely 5 liters of water be measured with two containers, one with 7-liter capacity and the other with 3-liter capacity? (The answer will be clear when you find it.)

SIMPLIFY

Perhaps the best advice for treating difficult problems is to *solve a simpler problem*. The basic idea is to remove or simplify some of the conditions until you can solve the simpler problem. Once the simpler problem is solved, you can reintroduce complications in steps until the full problem is done.

Solving a simpler problem is heavy weaponry in problem solving. It is often the easiest, and sometimes the only, way to crack intransigent problems. The process usually takes too much time to use on exams, but its use ranges from difficult assignments to fundamental research problems.

Example: A streetsweeper charges C dollars for the first quarter of a mile and S dollars for each additional quarter of a mile. Write an expression for the charge (in dollars) to sweep a street of X miles (where X is greater than 1 mile).

Solution: This is solved with a succession of simpler problems.

> Simpler Problem 1: Streetsweeper changes are S dollars for each mile. What is the charge for sweeping X miles?
> Answer 1: SX.
>
> Simpler Problem 2: Same as above but the charge is S dollars for each quarter mile.
> Answer 2: $4SX$.
>
> Original Problem: Now the charge for the first quarter mile is changed from S to C. Subtract S from the last answer and add C.
> Answer: $C - S + 4SX$

EXERCISE

Taxes are t dollars for every e dollars of income above \$3,000. Above \$60,000, income is taxed an additional 35 percent. Write an expression for the tax on an income of I dollars that is greater than \$60,000.
Answer: $t(I - 3,000)/e + .35 (I - 60,000)$.

Many kinds of problem elements can be simplified, including physical conditions, numbers, and the number of dimensions. A problem solver can find the speed of a cylinder as it rolls down a hill by first analyzing a cylinder that slides down the hill. Then it is obvious that the missing ingredient is rotational kinetic energy, and including this gives the full solution. Other problems may involve permutations and combinations (how many ways can ten students be assigned to twenty desks?). These become more transparent when the numbers are made small. In another case, the behavior of electrons in a crystal is understood by replacing the three-dimensional crystal with an artificial one-dimensional "periodic potential." Although these examples are too specialized to present in detail, they illustrate the wide applicability of solving-a-simpler-problem.

SUMMARY

Symbolize: Make a roster of symbols for all quantities in the problem. Symbols can be assigned numerical values or algebraic expressions. Use the roster to help determine the core equation—any central relation between the symbols.

Organize: Draw diagrams and write symbol lists. Organize solutions around a core equation. Undetermined symbols in the core condition are found from (1) a condition mentioned or implied in the problem statement or from (2) subordinate problems. When all quantities are expressed in terms of just one unknown, the problem is solved by substituting into the core equation.

Simplify: Reduce difficult problems to simpler ones that you can solve. Then add back the complexities in manageable stages.

21

■

TEACHING
WITH
TECHNIQUES

■

The techniques for learning
and remembering are
powerful teaching tools

■

Organization, visualization, and association accelerate learning and deepen memory—and the same principles can apply to teaching. In fact, several learning techniques can simply be inverted to create impressive teaching techniques.

You may agree that schools could boost learning dramatically and cost-effectively by giving a course in *Brainbooster* techniques. A study skills course such as this can be geared to any age level. It is an innovation that cannot disturb the established curriculum or impose upon teachers' academic freedom.

As usual, I must paint a large subject with a broad brush. Educators are aware of much that follows and many enlightened teachers use these methods routinely, without notice or fanfare. Nevertheless, I want to mention the factors that, in my opinion, are most important to good teaching. These methodologies also apply to teaching outside the classroom: teaching between parent and child, worker and coworker, professional and client.

THE HUMAN FACTOR

Human learning is profoundly influenced by personal factors. The most effective teachers give students respect, encouragement, and enthusiasm. Of course, it is easier to imagine that teaching is like programming a robot—that the information must be reduced to simple statements and fed into the student's empty brain. If teaching were simply this mechanical transmission of knowledge, virtually every knowledgeable person would be a good teacher. Sadly, this is not the case.

Your attitude is very important to your students, whether they are schoolchildren, coworkers, or clients. They want you to be approachable and genuinely concerned about them. Perhaps most of all, they want you to respect their abilities.

In a famous study, teachers were told that they had "bright" or "slow" students, although the classes actually were matched for equal abilities. Both groups were taught the same material and later tests confirmed that the "bright" students learned much more than the "slow" students. The labels were self-fulfilling.

The message is clear: when you genuinely respect your students, they share and meet your high expectations.

Throughout this book I extol the human potential—and surely your own experience with learning techniques is evidence that we all have immense untapped resources. This is as true for the deprived and learning handicapped as it is for gifted and talented individuals. Your students have impressive powers that deserve your admiration and respect.

Too many people regard praise and encouragement as peripheral or even extraneous to teaching. This is an understandable but mistaken view. There is a deep human need for approval, and it is a teaching tool you can use to great advantage. Conversely, try not to criticize students. Even when criticism is warranted, it is counterproductive. Try to excuse or see something right about any wrong answer. If a student gives an incorrect answer for a "good" reason, acknowledge its virtue and correct it. At times you may have to suppress impatience, but the results are worth it.

Humor is another teaching device that improves learning. Research has shown that students best remembered material that was presented with a touch of humor. Their recall of humorously treated material was even superior to that of heavily emphasized material. Here again, we see the human factors in learning. You don't want to act like a clown, but an occasional light touch is pleasant and good pedagogy.

TELESCOPIC TEACHING

A fetish for "logical order" can impede learning. Teachers and students alike naturally assume that step one must be fully mastered before they can progress to step two. If that were strictly true, however, no child could speak without first developing a comprehensive vocabulary and a good knowledge of grammar.

The point here is that serial ordering is not necessarily best for learning—most often, a telescopic approach is superior. We learn faster and better by first seeing a central objective in outline form. Only then are the associated details seen in proper perspective; careful definitions, fine points, and subordinate steps all relate to the core point.

Am I suggesting that teaching can begin at the middle or end of a topic? Emphatically, yes! The idea seems strange because we imagine knowledge is only built brick by brick, in a logical, methodical, and linear manner. We pretend that learning is like an exercise in geometry, where we begin with definitions and axioms and develop lemmas and theorems in a tight chain of logical steps. This is a quaint notion that has little to do with the actual working of the human mind. Even in geometry, a theorem is first seen (some say "intuited") in nearly complete form; only then are linear steps constructed to prove it.

Of course, difficult concepts or procedures must await a complete development to be fully grasped. Nevertheless, almost any concept can be simplified enough to give the learner a framework on which to build. A full description of *entropy* requires some knowledge of probability theory and logarithms, but almost anyone can appreciate that "entropy is a measure of the disorder in a system."

The telescopic approach to teaching is nicely illustrated by good newspaper reports. Major points are summarized in the first paragraph, and elaborations are added as the article progresses. Similarly, a course in world history would introduce Alexander the Great with a brief description of his impact on history. Only then would details of Alexander's life and battles be presented. The traditional approach is just the opposite—as though the story might be spoiled by hearing the ending.

Perhaps problem-oriented subjects suffer most from the

traditional linear approach. As lecturers plod through definitions and derivations, puzzled students plead to see an example. The students are right. When new concepts and principles are introduced in a transparent problem, students grasp the core of the theory. Refinements and elaborations then become meaningful and useful.

A telescopic approach to teaching should include, when possible, outlines and summaries of major units of instruction. These do not need to be detailed, but it is very desirable to let students know where they are going and where they have been.

Teaching requires planning and organization (even when it is spontaneous). Reveal your plans to your students. Clear objectives give purpose and direction to both the student and the instructor. Even more important, a student who knows the objectives has already learned a great deal.

DRESSING UP FACTS

Memorizing facts or terms is often dull and difficult. You can free students from this tedium by creating mnemonics with the techniques of visualization and association.

Students are familiar with acronyms and rhymes, but few are aware that visual associations are among the most powerful memory devices. Consequently, when you devise a visual mnemonic, you must instruct students to imagine the scene clearly and vividly.

You will find it more difficult to develop substitute images and associations for others than for yourself. When you create imagery for others, you cannot enjoy the complete freedom of your private thoughts or private meanings. Moreover, there are limits to how bizarre the associations may be, depending upon the sophistication of the students. These limitations can restrict your ability to create useful mnemonics.

Even with these restrictions, however, students can and do embrace quite imperfect substitute images. In an introductory art course, for example, early Greek columns are shown to have a three-part top or *capital*, consisting of *necking*, *echinus*, and *abacus*. The instructor told her students to visualize an animated column with small *caps* (for *capital*) attached to its *neck* (for *necking*), its *chin* (for *echinus*), and its *back* (for *abacus*). The students learned these, and a score of other architectural terms, shortly after hearing them.

USING EXAMPLES AND PARALLEL PROBLEMS

It is good policy to illustrate your subject matter with plenty of examples. Research shows that simple examples work better than complex examples—probably because complications obscure the central point. Accordingly, use the simplest examples that illustrate your objectives.

Although examples are desirable in almost any subject area, they are virtually indispensable in problem-oriented instruction. One way students learn to solve problems is to see others solve them. A teacher can demonstrate a problem solution and ask the students to do another, highly similar problem. The key words here are "highly similar." Most students need to concentrate on emulating your solution; new elements in the parallel problem can cause confusion.

You can usually create parallel problems by changing any inessential element in the original. For instance, you might change numbers, symbols, or vary the information given and sought. The problem "Find how long it takes for a ball to fall twenty meters from rest" can be converted to the parallel problem "Find how far a ball falls from rest in two seconds."

In both cases the principle and the relevant equation are the same.

Certainly, not all problems assigned to students should be parallel problems (except perhaps in elementary grades). Parallel problems do not test or extend students; rather, they provide practice in fundamentals and serve as models of good problem-solving technique.

TAKING SMALL STEPS

Chickens have been taught to dance! Not brilliant chickens—there are no brilliant chickens—but ordinary, barnyard hens have learned to turn and whirl on signal. The task was fragmented into tiny steps, and each step in the right direction was rewarded and reinforced. Ultimately, the sequence of steps completed the dance.

Many human learning objectives can also be broken into smaller, simpler objectives, and programmed instruction is predicated on such reductions. The technique is particularly effective for teaching computational and manipulative skills. For example, a martial arts instructor may teach an intricate kick by reducing it to component motions.

The small-step technique is illustrated here with a problem in the arithmetic of complex numbers:

Problem: Find the product $(a + ib)(a - ib)$, where a and b are real numbers and $i^2 = -1$.

$i^2 = ?$	answer: -1
$(2i)(2i) = ?$	answer: -4
$(2i)(3 + 2i) = ?$	answer: $6i - 4$
$(2i)(3 - 2i) = ?$	answer: $6i + 4$
$(3 + 2i)(3 - 2i) = ?$	answer: 13
$(a + bi)(a - bi) = ?$	answer: $a^2 + b^2$

Notice that each step is only a slight elaboration of the preceding step, and the sequence concludes with the original problem. Although the original problem may be difficult, the student should be able to perform each subordinate step.

This is a powerful approach, but it can be tedious and time-consuming. The small-step technique should therefore be limited to the more difficult or complex specific objectives.

QUESTIONING

Teaching is more effective when the instructor can establish a dialogue of questions and answers with students. Questioning has several features that make it a powerful tool.

Questioning requires students to take an active part throughout the session. Not surprisingly, research shows that learning improves with an increasing number of student responses.

Another virtue of continual dialogue is that students get immediate feedback—the desired answers are encouraged and others are discouraged.

Finally, the answers signal the instructor to adjust the approach to suit the students' needs. When a question appears too difficult, it can be simplified or broken into component parts. When a particular treatment is not working, an alternative can be chosen.

The technique of questioning is easily acquired. Simply ask students to perform any steps toward an objective that you expect are within their capability. You may feel no worthwhile purpose is served by asking questions that are easy to answer, but this is just the kind of exchange that creates student involvement. Of course, if the questioning is too trivial, time and energy are wasted. When this is the case, ask the students to handle more significant steps. You will quickly sense the right level.

Your questioning should not resemble a third-degree or an oral exam. Use a casual and gentle approach.

Questioning works both ways. Give students' questions your fullest attention. If a question seems foolish or heading in the wrong direction, help the student formulate the question in a useful way. Respect and encourage students' questions.

SUMMARY

The human factors: Consideration and respect for students are important elements in effective teaching. Encourage students with praise and approval. Occasional humor in teaching helps students to remember.

Telescopic teaching: Begin instruction with the most important idea or fact. Further refinements, details, and elaborations are then easily understood and retained. Reveal the organization of your teaching plans with outlines and summaries.

Dress facts: Develop visual mnemonics for isolated terms and facts.

Examples: Fully illustrate topics with examples. Simple examples are more effective than complex ones.

Parallel problems: Instruction in solving problems is assisted by demonstrating other, highly similar problems.

Small steps: Difficult objectives can be broken into a sequence of smaller, simple objectives.

Questioning: Ask questions frequently and keep the student involved as an active participant. Most questions should be relatively easy for the student to answer.

Index

Acronyms, 5
Asimov, Isaac, 114
Association, 9–11

Black Death, memory exercise about, 77–79
Borden, Gloria J., 68n
brain, 89–94
  hemisphere functions of, 91–92
  memory and, 92–94
  structure of, 89–91
Burger, Warren E., 58

Carnegie, Dale, 96
Chemical structures, as memory exercise, 104–10
  amino acids, 105–10
  diagram simplification, 106–9
  DNA, 104–5
  enzymes, 104–5

memorizing diagrams, 109–10
Core points, 60–65
  exercise, 61–62
  general idea, in thought maps, 60–61
  location of, 62
  specific idea, 61

Decision making, 147–51
  choice of options for, 149–50
  establishing criteria for, 148–49
  final synthesis in, 150–51
  goals and, 147–48

Elements of Style, 134
Energy: Resource, Slave, Pollutant, 43

Facts, dressing up of, 172–73
Frontal attack, 45–46

177